T0328606

Cambridge Elements ☰

Elements in Pragmatics
edited by
Jonathan Culpeper
Lancaster University, UK
Michael Haugh
University of Queensland, Australia

FICTION
AND PRAGMATICS

Miriam A. Locher
University of Basel

Andreas H. Jucker
University of Zurich

Daniela Landert
Heidelberg University

Thomas C. Messerli
University of Basel

CAMBRIDGE
UNIVERSITY PRESS

Shaftesbury Road, Cambridge CB2 8EA, United Kingdom

One Liberty Plaza, 20th Floor, New York, NY 10006, USA

477 Williamstown Road, Port Melbourne, VIC 3207, Australia

314–321, 3rd Floor, Plot 3, Splendor Forum, Jasola District Centre, New Delhi – 110025, India

103 Penang Road, #05–06/07, Visioncrest Commercial, Singapore 238467

Cambridge University Press is part of Cambridge University Press & Assessment, a department of the University of Cambridge.

We share the University's mission to contribute to society through the pursuit of education, learning and research at the highest international levels of excellence.

www.cambridge.org
Information on this title: www.cambridge.org/9781009095433

DOI: 10.1017/9781009091688

First published 2023

A catalogue record for this publication is available from the British Library.

ISBN 978-1-009-09543-3 Paperback
ISSN 2633-6464 (online)
ISSN 2633-6456 (print)

Fiction and Pragmatics

Elements in Pragmatics

DOI: 10.1017/9781009091688
First published online: February 2023

Miriam A. Locher
University of Basel

Andreas H. Jucker
University of Zurich

Daniela Landert
Heidelberg University

Thomas C. Messerli
University of Basel

Author for correspondence: Miriam A. Locher,

Abstract: This Element outlines current issues in the study of the pragmatics of fiction. It starts from the premise that fictional texts are complex and multilayered communicative acts which deserve attention in pragmatic research in their own right, and it highlights the need to understand them as cultural artefacts rich in possibilities to explore pragmatic effects and pragmatic theorising. The issues covered are (1) the participation structure of fictional texts, (2) the performance aspect of fictional texts, (3) the interaction between readers and viewers and the fictional texts, and (4) the pragmatic effects of drawing on indexical linguistic features for evoking ideologies in characterisation. This title is also available as Open Access on Cambridge Core.

Keywords: participation structure, performance, interaction, fiction, characterisation/identity construction

ISBNs: 9781009095433 (PB), 9781009091688 (OC)
ISSNs: 2633-6464 (online), 2633-6456 (print)

Contents

1 Introducing Fiction and Pragmatics

1.1 Setting the Scene

In this Element, we aim to make a strong case for using fictional data as one possible, and particularly rich, source for pragmatic theorising, and at the same time we make a strong case for using a pragmatic lens to gain new insights into fictional artefacts. We argue that a pragmatic perspective helps us to better understand the very nature of fictional data.

Important elements in exploring fiction are a clear understanding of the fictional contract between the creators of fiction and their recipients and an awareness of the complexities of the participation structure of fiction, both of which are fundamentally pragmatic notions because they are connected to the interpersonal nature of how we use language. The fictional contract is a silent agreement between all the people involved in the creation of a fictional artefact, such as authors, script writers and actors (i.e., the 'collective sender'; Dynel 2011), and their audiences, i.e., the readers or viewers. In order for fiction to work, they need to agree that the depicted characters and events are to be treated as fictitious (Locher & Jucker 2021: 16), even if the boundaries between the fictitious and the non-fictitious are sometimes explicitly negotiated or shifted, as in the case of books or films that are based on 'real events'. To understand this fictional contract, we need to be aware of the multiple levels of communication that are at work in a fictional artefact. On the one hand, this involves the intradiegetic level of communication, i.e., communication between the depicted characters ('diegesis' being the narrative). On the other hand, there is the extra-diegetic level of communication, i.e., the communication between the author and the audience. In plays or movies, this communication is mediated through actors, directors and entire production teams.

Many well-established concepts with wide reach and currency in pragmatics are crucial equally for fictional and non-fictional data; for instance, the concepts 'genre' or 'text type' and their relation to 'frames of expectations' and 'activity types'. In this book we primarily work with the concept of frame, defined as structure of expectations (cf. Goffman 1979; Locher & Jucker 2021: 61–3). If we treat fictional and non-fictional artefacts and performances as 'texts' and ultimately as data, we will discover the many analogies to non-fictional data in interpreting and sense-making processes. The concept of 'narrative', too, is an all-pervasive discourse unit, both in fictional and non-fictional instantiations, that helps individuals interpret their own and other people's life experiences. There are often fuzzy borders between fictional and non-fictional elements of narratives. Children, for example, are exposed to stories through oral narration, books and video-formats, and they engage in creating and populating story worlds through playing as well as retelling their own experiences.

There is also a clear connection to the field in linguistics that explores 'identity construction' (e.g., Bucholtz & Hall 2005; Davies & Harré 1990) and 'relational work', i.e., the work that people invest in creating, maintaining and challenging relationships (Locher 2008; Locher & Jucker 2021: ch. 8; Locher & Watts 2008). We argue that studying these concepts in fictional texts is useful in understanding them in general. When characters are created in a story world, they are assigned attributes through role and identity labels or character traits and also need to be given a voice and style of speaking. This characterisation works in connection with action, comportment, dress and the content of what they say. In combination, these cues give the character a shape in the minds of their readers/viewers/co-players, etc. Importantly, this character creation occurs in relation to the individual's life experience of what the indexicals (e.g., a word choice, an accent, a syntax pattern) stand for. These indexicals are thus linked to different types of (changing) norms on gender, age, ethnicity, etc., in their particular contexts. Recognising that there is no neutral reading/viewing is fundamental for engaging both with fiction and non-fiction. Focusing on the importance of authorial choices, Alvarez-Pereyre (2011: 62) argues in his often cited quotation that '[t]he very fact that the lexicogrammatical structures have been, *carefully and non-spontaneously*, chosen to fulfil the particular functions assigned, makes them extremely good specimens for the study of the relationships between forms, meanings and functions' (emphasis in original) in their particular context. In addition to this important insight, we stress and explore the co-construction of meaning by producers and audiences.

The same link to a person's horizon of interpretation can also be made with respect to the showing and telling of emotions. Recognising emotions and display rules for emotions in fiction might lead to sympathising and empathising with characters. For many, this is a fundamental motivation to engage with fictional artefacts in the first place. The field working on the signalling of emotional stance can thus be drawn on when interpreting fiction, and we can learn from fiction how emotions are staged.

There is no one-way street from non-fictional to fictional data. It is entirely possible that life experience and knowledge about real-life contexts is gained and accumulated by engaging with fiction, rather than the other way around. This is not only true for the display of emotions but also for knowledge of genre and text type, linguistic indexicals and norms, etc.

The usefulness of pragmatic concepts for the interpretation of fiction is vast, and this potential has long been recognised in the fields of literary and cultural studies, stylistics, and pragmatics (e.g., among many, Bednarek 2018; Chapman & Clark 2014, 2019; Culpeper 2001; Culpeper et al. 1998; Leech & Short 2007; Stockwell & Whiteley 2014). In this Element, we can neither replace nor summarise this work or our own previous work in the form of a handbook (Locher & Jucker 2017), text book (Locher & Jucker 2021) or past and current research endeavours (e.g., Landert 2021a; Messerli 2021). However, we wish to acknowledge the breadth of the field and turn readers to the sources above for areas that we cannot cover and pragmatic concepts that we cannot introduce in detail with respect to how they might apply to fiction (e.g. conversational implicature, speech act theory, relevance theory). Instead, we will draw on our work and other scholars' insights in order to explore those four areas further which we deem to hold particular potential for advancing insights into both pragmatics and fiction, as outlined in Section 1.2.

1.2 Outline of the Element

We wish to shed light on four fields of research, with the aim of exploring how pragmatic theorising and fiction can be brought together and to hopefully entice more scholars to work in them:

– participation structure (Section 2)
– performance (Section 3)
– interaction (Section 4) and
– discourse and ideologies through character creation (Section 5)

Each section contains a brief introduction to the respective concept in linguistics, followed by three sections that develop and explore the concept with respect to three different types of fictional data:

– written fiction
– performed fiction
– telecinematic fictional artefacts

The distinctions between these three types of fiction are not always clear-cut, but we use 'written fiction' to refer to formats such as novels, short stories and poems. Such formats often include dialogues between the fictitious characters, but they also regularly include descriptive passages. Typically, written fictional artefacts are consumed by readers who read a printed text, but poems are often recited, and many novels are turned into audiobooks. In these forms, and for the purpose of our rough and ready classification, they still count as written fiction. Performed fiction according to our classification consists of fictional artefacts that are performed by artists on a stage in front of a live audience. This includes both improvised theatre, in which the actors spontaneously invent characters, scenes and events in the course of the performance, and plays in which the actors perform a text written by an author. The term 'telecinematic artefacts' encompasses both artefacts that are produced for the small screen (e.g., the television) and for the cinema (Piazza et al. 2011). Telecinematic fictional artefacts are similar to performed fiction in that they also rely on actors who perform characters, scenes and events, but in this case the performance has been recorded and is being viewed by the audience at a later time.

The three datasets thus differ on several levels. First, the medium of transmission differs from written, live performed, to 'frozen' telecinematic artefacts. Second, there are different interaction possibilities and spaces opened up. For example, there are different readings over time and different reception communities, such as discourse communities, fandoms, affinity spaces, live performance, audience interaction, or live viewing contexts such as commenting during a movie performance or during online watch parties. Finally, the means of expressing multimodal interaction differ. In written fiction, action is described (telling mode) and performed through dialogue (showing mode), while performed types of fiction can draw on multimodal cues to construct action and interaction (speech, action, appearance, music, camera angles and more).

Discussing the three data sets in each of the sections dedicated to a particular pragmatic phenomenon will shed light on its complexity. In Section 2, on the participation structure, we introduce the complex communicative settings of fictional artefacts. These are typically produced by groups of individuals with different roles in the production process, and they are addressed to large and heterogeneous audiences. We build on the existing models, and focus in particular on their dynamic aspects, by pointing out how fictional artefacts not only respond to different types of readers or viewers but how they actively create different audiences, and how the artefact itself is shaped and modified through its specific participation structure. We show the respective commonalities between written, performed and telecinematic fiction, and we highlight some of their crucial differences. We also identify some potential areas of future pragmatically informed research on the dynamics of the participation structure of fictional artefacts.

The entire spectrum of fictional artefacts – from written and static to performed and improvised – consists of (multimodal) texts that are put on display for an audience. In Section 3, on performance, we discuss how the careful design of fictional artefacts for their effect on the audience influences the use of language. We cover features of orality in written fiction, the deliberate staging of spoken language in performed fiction, the display of skills by text producers and the role of multimodal compositions in telecinematic fiction. The section builds on Section 2, which is on participation structure, by looking at how text producers compose fictional artefacts for an audience.

Section 4, on interaction, builds on Sections 2 and 3 on participation structure and performance by exploring to what extent fictional texts can become dynamic and interactional. In written fiction, we focus on the engagement of texts with their authors as well as with other texts. In performed fiction, we highlight the audience's uptake and co-construction of meaning (especially in improvised theatre with viewer input). In telecinematic fiction, we foreground the viewers' interaction with the artefact in practices such as writing spin-offs, translation by and for the community, and posting reviews and comments to audiovisual artefacts.

Section 5, on characterisation and ideologies, explores how fictional characters are created with the help of linguistic and multimodal indexicals. In addition to appearance and action, which define characters in fictional texts, authors can exploit the indexical force of grammatical, lexical and phonological features to construct belonging (e.g., variations in region/class/age/gender). Section 5 explores how this can be done and links it to participation structure, performance and interaction, discussed in Sections 2, 3 and 4. Section 5 also discusses the interface of discourse analysis and pragmatics in that the indexicals are tied to ideologies that are particular to a given time and place.

Finally, in Section 6, we first reflect on the four key concepts that guided our discussions in this book: participation structure, performance, interaction and characterisation, which evokes ideologies. Section 6 concludes by raising additional issues that can further explorations of fiction through a pragmatic lens and our theorising of pragmatics through fictional data. Throughout the Element, we draw on fiction written in English to illustrate our points. This choice is due to our background in English linguistics and literary and cultural studies.

2 Participation Structure

2.1 Towards a Dynamic Model of Participation Structure

'Participation structure' is a concept that captures 'who interacts with whom on what levels' (Locher & Jucker 2021: 451). When we think of communication, we tend to think in terms of two people who talk to each other and take turns in being speaker and listener, but in many cases, things are clearly more complex. Back in 1979, Goffman pointed out that we need to distinguish between different speaker roles: the 'principal', whose ideas are communicated; the 'author', who drafts the words with which the ideas are communicated and the 'animator', who utters the words. In 'canonical talk', as Goffman (1979: 16) calls it, the three roles are combined in one individual who utters their own words on behalf of themselves, but the roles are clearly separated in the case of newsreaders or spokespersons reading out what somebody else has written on behalf of an institution. He also distinguished clearly between a number of different recipient roles – addressee, auditor, overhearer and eavesdropper – who differ from each other to the extent to which they are directly addressed, ratified or even known to be there at all by the speaker. Bell (1991) extended Goffman's insights to account more systematically for mass media communication, and more recently, these models have been adapted and modified to account for the complexity of fictional communication (Bubel 2008; Dynel 2011; Leech & Short 2007; Locher & Jucker 2021; Messerli 2017). They work with different sender roles, different recipient roles and multiple embeddings of what is communicated between the sender and the recipient. Viewers of telecinematic artefacts, for instance, are conceptualised as overhearers or ratified listeners (Bubel 2008; Dynel 2011, 2017). Locher and Jucker (2021: ch. 3) propose a model of communication for performed fiction which extends the complexity even further (see Figure 1).

This model recognises the complexity of the production team that is necessary to turn the ideas of the author and the scriptwriters into a telecinematic artefact which can be enjoyed by a large and heterogeneous audience, which may consist not only of regular viewers who are familiar with its specific genre and perhaps previous episodes and seasons but also of critics with a professional interest in the artefact, incidental recipients who are less familiar with the specific type of film and accidental recipients who should not even be there, for example children watching an X-rated movie. The model also recognises the communicative complexity of the artefact itself, with depicted interactions between characters on the intradiegetic level and the communicative interaction with a studio audience (real or in the form of canned laughter) on what Locher and Jucker (2021: 53) call the supradiegetic level.

In this section, we build on this model and extend it by focusing on its dynamic aspects. All the models mentioned above, including the model by Locher and Jucker (2021), seem to suggest an independent existence of the creators, the artefact and the different types of recipients. Here, we argue in addition that they should be understood as discursively and dynamically constructed.

The model depicted in Figure 1 appears to suggest that the audience is segregated into more or less clearly separated circles of viewers, and that the creators take these circles into consideration when they produce the artefact. Here we stress the way in which the artefact itself not only responds to these differences but actually creates them (Brock 2015). From a more static perspective, we would perhaps focus on the ways in which the creators of

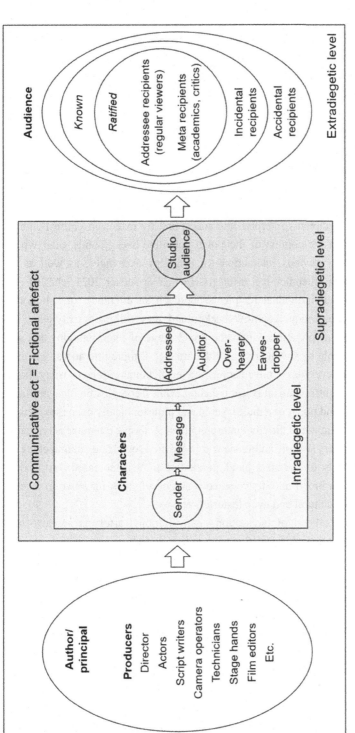

Figure 1 A model of telecinematic communication of performed fiction (reproduced from Locher & Jucker 2021: 53)

a telecinematic artefact take the different types of viewers into consideration and add specific details that are intended for regular viewers, such as allusions or jokes that would be lost on incidental recipients, or for incidental viewers, in the form of brief recaps of what happened before. From a dynamic perspective, we also analyse the ways in which the artefact itself creates such audiences by integrating or excluding certain viewers. As we will see in Sections 2.2 to 2.5, such dynamic processes can also be observed in other forms of fiction, not only in movies and television series.

The fictional artefacts themselves should also be seen as dynamically created in the sense that their meaning, like utterances in a casual conversation, is essentially made up of the communicative efforts of the sender and the processing effort of the recipient. Recipients interpret utterances, and by extension entire fictional artefacts, against the context of their own cognitive backgrounds, their world views and their previous interactions in everyday exchanges, as well as in interactions with other fictional artefacts (Locher & Jucker 2021: ch. 10). To the extent that all individual recipients approach an utterance, or a fictional artefact, with their unique cognitive background, they will necessarily come up with a unique interpretation within the broad range of interpretations that are evoked as possible by the utterance or the artefact. Simple utterances, whether they occur in everyday conversations or in fictional artefacts, may have a relatively straightforward and clear meaning, while a complex fictional artefact, such as a profound poem or a multilayered and philosophically deep movie, will allow for a large range of different interpretations. A simple utterance is typically produced for a very specific addressee within a shared social and cultural context. Fictional artefacts, on the other hand, in addition to their increased complexity, typically reach a broad and heterogeneous audience which may live in a very different social, cultural and even historical context.

On a different level of interaction, many fictional artefacts are also co-produced by the creators and the recipients in a more tangible way, as for instance in the case of a theatre production in which the actors adjust their performance on the basis of how the audience responds to their playing, or a television series which integrates fan forum suggestions into subsequent episodes and seasons. And on yet another level, some fictional artefacts are actually co-produced by creator and recipient so that the two roles appear to blur into each other. For instance, this is the case in some forms of jointly produced texts or reader responses to fan fiction which become integral parts of the fictional artefact itself (see Section 4). In the following sections, we build on the dynamic aspects of the model of participation structure depicted in Figure 1 to explain their application to written fiction, theatre performances and tele-cinematic artefacts.

2.2 Written Fiction

The participation structure that obtains for prose fiction appears to be considerably simpler than the one for telecinematic communication depicted in Figure 1. An author of a novel or a short story does not need an entire team of actors, directors, camera operators, sound engineers and so on to bring the fictional artefact to life. However, even in the case of prose fiction, the participation structure is more complex than might appear at first sight, and it involves numerous elements that are best understood from a dynamic perspective. Let us take the novel *Americanah* by the celebrated Nigerian writer Chimamanda Ngozi Adichie as an example. It begins with the following sentences (Extract 2.1):

Extract 2.1 *Americanah* (Adichie 2013: 1)

Princeton, in the summer, smelled of nothing, and although Ifemelu liked the tranquil greenness of the many trees, the clean streets and stately homes, the delicately overpriced shops, and the quiet, abiding air of earned grace, it was this, the lack of a smell, that most appealed to her, perhaps because the other American cities she knew well had all smelled distinctly. Philadelphia had the musty scent of history. New Haven smelled of neglect. Baltimore smelled of brine, and Brooklyn of sun-warmed garbage. But Princeton had no smell.

In these opening sentences, we get to know what will turn out to be the main character and focaliser of this novel, Ifemelu, and we get to know a few of her characteristic features, for instance her keen sense of perception and her engagement with American cities. On a more basic – and rather trivial – level, these opening sentences also make it clear that we are dealing with a novel written in English, which already defines the potential audience of this book as one who reads English. But, in fact, these opening sentences are, of course, not the beginning of the interaction of a potential reader with the fictional artefact. They are preceded by textual elements that Genette (1997) called the paratext, that is to say elements such as the cover of the book, including its artwork, the author's name, the title of the book and so on, followed by the front matter, with its detailed copyright information, a dedication, a preface and so on. From a pragmatic perspective, they are part of the overall message that readers hold in their hands and that might influence the ways in which they interpret the novel.

The author may have very limited control of the paratext, but there are additional layers of communicative elements over which the author has even less control. The first contact of a potential reader with the book may have been, for instance, a recommendation by a friend, a review in a newspaper, an electronic recommendation from a book vendor based on the previous reading history of the reader, a book display in a bookshop or an entry on a list of required readings for a class at university. These framings, if they lead the potential reader to become an actual reader, may well influence the reading experience in quite significant ways. They may create certain frames of expectations for the book and thus become part of what is communicated to the reader, even if the reader ultimately decides that the framing had been inaccurate or misleading.

Webpages of online booksellers provide a wealth of information for each book that is called up through a search or a click on an appropriate link. It typically includes a picture of the book cover, a brief synopsis of the book, information on the author, endorsements from published reviews, lists of similar books, sales rankings and reader reviews. From a marketing perspective, all these elements are meant to increase the satisfaction of customers by helping them to reach an informed decision about the advertised product. And needless to say, they are also meant to increase the sales figures and the profits of the supplier. From a pragmatic perspective, however, these elements are interesting because they present the fictional artefact in a certain way. They shape the reading expectations and therefore the reading experience of the people who decide to purchase the book. In the case of Adichie's *Americanah*, some of the reader reviews frame the novel as a love story between the star-crossed lovers Ifemelu and Obinze; others see it more as a coming-of-age story or as a treatise on race in the United States and Nigeria. Some reviewers indicate that they loved it and others describe it as disappointing or boring. All these opinions and framings may, in one way or another, not only influence potential readers to actually purchase the book but also the way in which they read the novel.

As an illustration, let us have a closer look at the book cover of Adichie's *Americanah* and how it helps to shape and frame the reader's expectations and reading experience. As a very successful novel that has won a number of important literary prizes, it is sold in several different editions with different book covers, but all of them contain not only the author's name and the title of the book but also typically mention one or more of the prizes won by the novel, one of the author's earlier novels and, most prominently, they provide endorsements in the form of short phrases picked out of published reviews. For example, consider the compilation in Extract 2.2.

Extract 2.2 *Americanah* (Adichie 2013): various book covers; reproduced as in original

- 'A tour de force' Mail on Sunday
- 'Dazzling. . . . Funny and defiant, and simultaneously so wise. . . . Brilliant.'
  – San Francisco Chronicle
- 'A DELICIOUS, IMPORTANT NOVEL' THE TIMES
- 'ALERT, ALIVE AND GRIPPING' INDEPENDENT

– 'SOME NOVELS TELL A GREAT STORY AND OTHERS MAKE YOU
CHANGE THE WAY YOU LOOK AT THE WORLD. *AMERICANAH*
DOES BOTH' GUARDIAN

Most covers prefer abstract cover designs, but one uses a full-bleed picture (i.e., filling the entire space of the cover) of a young, black woman in profile. It is, of course, difficult to assess the full extent to which the graphic design and the mention of prizes, previous novels and endorsements actually influence the decisions of potential readers to purchase the book and read it, but it is clear that these elements are part of a complex communicative situation. It is not only Chimamanda Ngozi Adichie who communicates her text to an audience. The book itself is the product of a large team who created it, including editors, typesetters, graphic designers, marketing specialists and so on. In addition, when it reaches a potential reader, it may have been framed by a large number of contexts which all may – to some extent at least – influence the reader's reading experience and thus become part of the product. Adichie is the author of the novel, but her voice is embedded in contextual voices, and these contextual voices even include reader voices, in the form of endorsements, reviews and recommendations. Thus, the readers do not only approach this fictional artefact with their highly individual cognitive backgrounds and previous reading experiences, but each of them is faced with an individually framed and contextualised artefact.

The fictional artefact, in this case the novel *Americanah*, therefore, in a crucial sense is not a static product, but it is a dynamic entity which is created by the readers in their reading process. This reading process is shaped not only by the book itself and the personality of the readers, with all their previous reading and life experiences, but also by the expectations that are created by the book and its paratext, and by its wider communicative context, such as personal recommendations, professional advertising material, book reviews, sales rankings and customer reviews on the website of an online bookseller. It is also dynamic in its shapeshifting potential. Novels may not only exist in different editions (hardcover, paperback, e-book, audiobook, UK or US edition, etc.) but they may also be turned into plays or movies. Simplified versions may be created for children or non-native speakers and so on. Books, in particular children's books, may be read out for a listening audience, and e-readers may offer seamless switches between a text version and an audiobook version. Translations provide new versions of an artefact, and they are never identical to the original but only similar. And readers who re-read a novel are likely to have a reading experience that differs considerably from a first reading.

Thus, the participation structure for printed fiction must be appreciated in all its complexity, which goes far beyond a simple artefact created by an author for a specific audience. The actual author is certainly the primary source of the artefact but the product that is consumed by the audience is embedded in several additional communicative layers which all add specific framings and, therefore, meanings, and every single member of the audience creates, or rather re-creates, the artefact for themselves.[1]

2.3 Performed Fiction

The participation structure of performed fiction shares most of the complexities of written fiction described above. For instance, in the case of scripted drama, each member of the audience will approach a performed play with different frames of expectations, which may have been shaped through advertising materials, critical reviews of the performance, familiarity with adaptations of the play, previous readings and viewings of this and other plays, and previous productions by the director and the theatre company. Especially in the case of classic plays, like Shakespeare's, it is quite common to watch different productions of the same play, and even audience members who see a play performed for the first time are likely to have encountered numerous references to the play, its plot or the text itself before. Thus, just like in written fiction, the reception of a performance varies across members of the audience depending on their degree of familiarity with and expectations of the play.

Apart from these similarities, the participation structure of performed fiction differs from written fiction in a number of ways. For instance, in contrast to written fiction, performed fiction is enacted. Actors take the role of animators, providing a voice, physicality, gestures and facial expressions to the dialogue, all of which add further layers of meaning to the text. The play is presented in spoken form, which means that intonation contour, loudness, pitch, speed, pauses and overlaps convey information as well. As a consequence, the study of the pragmatics of (video recordings of) performed fiction can differ considerably from the study of written play texts. While it is certainly possible to focus on written transcriptions of performed dialogue only, a multimodal analysis including sound and image will provide relevant additional information on how meaning is communicated to the audience.

One apparent characteristic of performed fiction is that, typically, the audience is present during the performance. Remote viewings of performed fiction are possible both as live streams and in the form of recordings, but the live audience is what sets performed fiction apart from most other forms of fiction.

---

[1] This does not mean that there are no similar interpretations of fictional artefacts possible, but it highlights that the process is created within individuals who are embedded in a particular cultural space and time.

Sharing a space means that each audience member's experience of the performance is shaped by the reactions of other audience members, which can include laughter, gasps, emotional sounds, applause, comments or even people falling asleep or leaving the venue. While access to audience responses can also be provided for other forms of fiction (see, e.g., Locher & Messerli 2020; Messerli & Locher 2021 on timed comments in online streaming platforms of telecinematic artefacts; see also Section 4), sharing the same physical space at the same time creates a different kind of involvement. In addition, the presence of the audience during the performance makes it possible for audience responses to influence the performance, a point that we will discuss in more detail in Section 4.

Another difference between performed and written fiction concerns the production process and the roles of the text producers. In the case of performances of scripted plays, the playwright is the first author and principal, providing the original words and message of the play. However, each production of a play involves a new interpretation of the text through the director, the actors, stage and costume designers, make-up artists and everyone else who is involved. Thus, the roles of author and principal are shared between the playwright and the theatre company. This distribution of roles is similar to telecinematic fiction, where authorship is shared by screenwriters, directors and other producers, as shown in Figure 1. However, for the performance of scripted plays, such co-authorships can span several centuries or even millennia. For instance, a British theatre company performing Sophocles' play *Antigone* (Sophocles 2000) in 2022 will reinterpret a text that was written almost 2,500 years ago in a different cultural context and in a different language. Irrespective of whether the company decides on a modern adaptation or on staying close to the original text, the audience will always perceive the performance through different layers of contextualisation, where more recent events invite new interpretations of the classic text.

The participation structure of improvised theatre is different from that of scripted theatre in some crucial respects (Landert 2021a). For instance, for improvised theatre, the roles of author, principal and animator fall together. Each performer of an improvised play continuously decides on the play's plot and message, the wording of the lines and how to present them. Put differently, performers in improvised plays simultaneously occupy the role of a playwright, director and actor (Harvard & Wahlberg 2017: 13). At the same time, the authorship of the text is shared between performers, with each performer authoring the lines they speak. This results in a co-authored text in which the ideas and language choices of different producers are woven together line by line, not unlike in spontaneous conversation. From a pragmatic point of view, this makes it possible to study the collaborative creation of fiction in a setting in which the authorship of each utterance is known to the researcher.

In terms of production process, there is no delay between text authoring and audience reception for improvised theatre. While the audience of Sophocles' *Antigone* listens to lines written thousands of years ago, the audience of an improvised play hears lines that are created in this moment. As a consequence, improvised theatre can integrate references to the here and now. For instance, performers may refer to current events in general, a recent sports game or social media hype, the weather, and even to anything that is happening in the theatre during the performance. In a performance by the improviser duo *MOLLY* (Susan Messing and Norm Holly), the ventilation in the room turned on during a pause in the dialogue. The performer, Susan Messing, integrated the noise into the fictional text by turning it into the sound of a nearby electrical plant, which had not been mentioned in the performance so far (see Extract 2.3).

Extract 2.3 *MOLLY* (2021), 24 October, 7:34–7:42

oh you hear the plant next door?
that's the-
that's the electrical plant.
next door.
which might be interrupting your quiet time.

Integrating references to the present time and place into the fictional world is specific to improvised fiction. As a form of metafictional frame-breaking, the strategy crosses the boundary between the fictional world and the extradiegetic world, which can create audience involvement as well as humour (Landert 2021a: 75–7). Similar effects can be created through direct address of the audience, a strategy that is known as 'breaking the fourth wall' and which will be discussed in more detail in Section 4.3.

The embedding of the performed text in the here and now presents special challenges for research. In order to study performed fiction, researchers often rely on recordings of performances. Recordings are usually carried out in such a way that the language of performers is clearly audible, which means that lavalier or directional microphones are used that filter out noise from the auditorium. In Extract 2.3, the humming of the ventilation on the recording is so subtle that it would be very easy to miss if one was not present during the performance. Likewise, references to recent events and shared local context can be hard to identify and understand. Given that the performers usually create fiction for an audience that is co-present and local, such references are often left unexplained and can be difficult to resolve for a researcher who does not share the same background as the audience.

The final characteristic that sets improvised theatre apart from scripted theatre, written fiction and telecinematic fiction is the fact that improvisation does not provide any options for planning, revising and editing the text offline. Written texts and telecinematic fiction can be revised and corrected any number of times before they are published, and the audience only sees the final version, which was approved by the production team. For scripted theatre, the performance of the play is preceded by a rehearsal process in which different options of presenting the play are tried out, selected and perfected. Norrthon (2019) presents a very detailed study of how the performance of eight lines of Lucy Prebble's play *The Effect* (2016) by Riksteatern is developed over a rehearsal period of forty-five days, affecting wording, gestures, pauses and overlaps. Once the play is performed, there may still be minor changes from performance to performance, but the decisions of how to stage these lines result from an extensive rehearsal process. In contrast, performers in improvised theatre cannot practise and revise their lines. They need to respond in the moment, and the only option for editing their lines is through online self- and other-repairs. For researchers of improvised theatre, this presents ample opportunities for studying how performers respond to potential problems in the performance, such as slips of the tongue and misunderstandings.

To sum up, the participation structure of performed fiction is even more complex than that of written fiction. For both scripted and improvised theatre, the multimodal enactment of the text adds further layers of meaning to the text, and the co-presence of the audience during the performance needs to be taken into account when studying how performed fiction is perceived by the audience. For scripted theatre, the potential of temporal and cultural distance between the composition of the play by the playwright and its staging can complicate the analysis further. For improvised fiction, complications can arise from a highly localised contextualisation of the performance, which may not always be fully accessible to the researcher.

2.4 Telecinematic Fiction

Our categorisation of fiction into written, performed and telecinematic implies a focus for each type at a particular stage in the process that defines fiction-as-communication. If written communication is identified by the writing of fiction (even though plays are also written), and performed fiction by its performance (even though novels can be performed as scenic readings), then telecinematic fiction is defined by its telecinematicity, and in particular by the distance (encoded in Greek *tele*) between filming (performance) and viewing (reception). This distance is bridged with the help of some sort of technological apparatus that affords the collective sender the means of writing a complex multimodal text to film, video or some form of digital storage and allows the recipients to later view and listen to the artwork in a post-produced (edited, mixed, enhanced with digital effects, etc.) and finalised version. It is partially the complex production apparatus that makes the production of telecinematic fiction a particularly collaborative endeavour, whereas its reception can be either akin to that of performed fiction, as when audiences go to a movie theatre, or similar to reading written fiction, for example when viewers stream an episode of a TV series on their phone and watch it alone. While we examine these processes in more detail in Section 4, where we explore the interaction between authors and recipients, they are of importance also for the communicative setting of fictional film and television more generally.

For telecinematic fiction as a whole, the pragmatic literature has modelled and discussed participation structures in some detail (see, e.g., Section 2.1; Bubel 2006, 2008; Brock 2015; Locher & Jucker 2021; Messerli 2017). Less attention has been paid so far to the individual settings that communicative processes in telecinematic fiction give rise to. When scholars of pragmatics inevitably turn to the role of participants at each stage of film- and television-making and viewing, they will arrive at questions in line with the following non-exhaustive list:

a) How do **scriptwriters** transform imagined multimodality to writing on the page or screen?
b) What role do directors, cinematographers, actors, etc. play when performing on a set during **filming**?
c) What meaning is added, changed or edited in other ways during **post-production** by editors, effect artists, composers of the film score, etc.?
d) What additional layers of meaning are added when telecinematic fiction is made accessible to additional audiences, be it through audio description for visually impaired viewers, intralingual subtitling for the hard of hearing, or translation processes such as dubbing, voice-over or interlingual subtitling?
e) What role do viewers play when engaging with any version of a telecinematic artefact and how do they arrive at meaning?

The goal of this section is not to answer each of these questions or discuss the respective research areas in great detail, but to illustrate here some of the exemplary applications and research avenues that questions (a)–(c) will lead to. We will return to questions (d) and (e) throughout the subsequent sections, but in particular in Sections 3.4, 4.4 and 5.4.

(a) Scriptwriters

Given the large number of actual roles that make up the collective sender of telecinematic fiction, it would take at least a full-length monograph to describe each role in film-as-communication in full. However, given our focus on linguistic meaning-making and the inclusion of a section on written fiction in Sections 2, 3, 4 and 5, it is important to address the scriptwriting process of film – a process that has so far received very little attention in research within the pragmatics of fiction, the notable exception being Bednarek (2018, 2019). Generally, scriptwriters are either used as an example of what the collective sender consists of (as we have done in Section 2.1), or they are mentioned in the context of character development (e.g., Bednarek 2011). While Bednarek's (2018, 2019) important contributions have started to fill this lacuna in linguistic research of telecinematic fiction, they are employed teleologically: the process of scriptwriting, described on the basis of interviews with television script writers and surveys of screenwriting manuals, is included as an explanatory tool to better understand the shape of the telecinematic text as a product. This leaves unexplored avenues of research that address film scripts – the written fiction that telecinematic fiction is based on – as texts in their own right, situated in a particular participation structure. In addition, film and television scripts could lend themselves to contrastive studies between script and resulting film, between novel and adapted script, or between comparable plays and scripts. The question in each case could be how the difference in settings, including audience, involved participants, communicative affordances and conventions, affects the resulting language.

Another interesting comparison concerns stage directions in plays and in screenplays. Whereas plays are often also published and read as literary texts, screenplays are more typically used as functional texts that inform and instruct a professional readership, the director and cast, in their performance for the camera. In line with this difference in audience design we could ask, for instance, if stage directions in either text are different in style and content, perform different functions and discursively construct different readerships. Another difference in reception settings worth exploring is the fact that well-known plays are restaged and reinterpreted many times, whereas screenplays are prototypically frozen into only one finalised performance.[2] This, too, is likely to have effects on how scripts for films and plays are written.

---

[2] Apart from the one performance that survives as part of the final film, there are of course, on occasion, other enactments of film script scenes that are seen by a wider public. Examples are out-takes included in the end credits of films, as extras included on optical media or offered alongside the main artefact on streaming sites; alternative versions of films, such as extended editions or director cuts; and shot-for-shot remakes like Van Sant's *Psycho* (1998), an adaptation of Hitchcock's classic *Psycho* (1960).

(b) Filming

To study the filming or production of telecinematic fiction is to look at its performance, to which Section 3 is dedicated. We therefore address only one particular performative aspect here and refer to Section 3.4 for further details.

To our knowledge, no studies in pragmatics have so far looked empirically at the specific processes of performance during filming outside of what is ultimately captured on camera. Apart from actors' use of language and interaction with the camera, topics of pragmatic interest in this arena include communication between the director (who typically has most of the creative control), cinematography (main cinematographer and assistants who together have control of the camera) and actors, to name but the three most prominent examples of cast and crew. Interaction among them is particularly interesting because the actors' performance at the centre of everyone's shared attention is directly embodied and experienced by the actors, actively received and captured by the cinematography, and directed, controlled and conceptually framed by the director. Common ground must be established based on shared repertoire, including professional knowledge about filmmaking and familiarity with the screenplay; specific roles are in part institutional and in part negotiated in situ as part of the mutual engagement on the film set; and the interaction is centred around the joint enterprise of creating a film. In other words, one area of pragmatic research in this arena is the understanding of situated language use among the film's cast and crew, understood as a community of practice (see Lave & Wenger 1991; Wenger 2002).

(c) Post-production

If the making of telecinematic fiction is conceptualised as a form of speaking, and the filmmakers as speakers, we can characterise scriptwriting, filming and post-production as processes governed by principals, authors and animators, using Goffman's terms (Section 2.1). From the point of view of the recipients, a telecinematic artefact as a whole speaks on behalf of a principal often called the collective sender, authored by scriptwriters and directors, and animated not by actors alone but by the whole production process, of which the embodied interactions of actors are but one important part. Post-production processes, called the 'assembly stage' by Bordwell et al. (2020), are a part of telecinematic discourse that is often overlooked. They include the work of picture and sound editors in finalising the shapes of scenes, their sequence and transitions, or that of composers creating the musical score that accompanies many telecinematic artefacts. After utterances have been phrased by scriptwriters and directors and performed jointly by actors and the filming crew, an often lengthy process of authorial decision about the final shape of utterances and the performance more generally still follows.

The importance of post-production for telecinematic meaning-making is particularly evident in the case of some of the most commercially successful films – *Avatar* (2009) or any of Marvel's *Avenger* movies are examples – in which characters and parts of the mise en scène were never in front of a camera, but added digitally afterwards. Even in films without digital effects, post-production can alter dramatically what telecinematic artefacts ultimately say to their recipients: endings are changed (e.g., *The Cabinet of Dr. Caligari* (1920) or *Brazil* (1985)), voice-overs are added or removed (e.g., the theatric and director's cuts of *Blade Runner* (1982)), characters become less talkative (e.g., Geralt of Rivia in the first season of *The Witcher* (2019)) or are removed from the story altogether (e.g., actress Tracey Ullman's character in *Death Becomes Her* (1992)); single actors play several characters and interact with themselves (e.g., Lindsay Lohan playing Annie and Hallie in *The Parent Trap* (1998), a Hollywood adaptation of Kästner's (2015) *Lisa and Lottie*); studio audience laughter is included to indicate where humour is intended (see Messerli 2016, 2021). While post-production itself thus deserves attention from pragmatic scholarship, it is important to note that its existence has (pragmatic) impact on other stages of film- and television-making and on other communication processes. For instance, actors' performances may be affected because they interact not with other actors but either with stand-ins or with imaginary interlocutors in front of a green screen; the setting more generally is bound to change if it is not constrained by what can be recorded photographically; substantial re-edits are often informed by test-screenings; post-production may also lead to re-shoots and thus the addition of further performances in front of the cameras to the final film; and, since all of these aspects shape the artefact that viewers see, reception processes, too, are affected by post-production.

2.5 Summary

In this section, we have highlighted the pragmatic complexities of communication through fictional artefacts. In all three forms of fiction – written, performed and telecinematic – the multilayered aspects of senders, recipients and the artefact itself need to be teased apart very carefully for a pragmatically adequate description, and they have to be understood as dynamic entities which mutually impact each other.

However, in the context of this section, we could no more than scratch the surface and hint at some of the important differences across the different types of fiction. Much more research needs to be carried out for a more comprehensive understanding of the discursive construction of sender, recipient and artefact in written, performed and telecinematic fiction. In Sections 3 and 4, we will return to some of these issues when we discuss the pragmatic positioning of fictional artefacts in the interaction between senders and recipients.

3 Performance

3.1 Introducing Research Avenues into Performance and Fiction

In a narrow sense of the term, performance can be applied to a subgroup of fictional artefacts that are performed in front of live audiences. This is how we use the term when referring to performed fiction in contrast to written fiction and telecinematic fiction. However, in a wider sense of the term, performance can be used to refer to certain aspects that characterise all fictional artefacts. In this wider use, performance emphasises that fiction is created for an audience and that the language in fictional artefacts – alongside other modes of expression – is carefully designed for its effect on the audience. In Bauman's words:

> [P]erformance is understood as a special mode of situated communicative practice, resting on the assumption of accountability to an audience for a display of communicative skill and efficacy. In this sense of performance, the act of expression is put on display, objectified, marked out to a degree from its discursive surroundings and opened up to interpretive scrutiny and evaluation by an audience. Performance foregrounds form-function-meaning interrelationships through verbal display. (Bauman 2000: 1)

Even though all fiction is performative in this sense, the role of language varies across different types of fictional artefacts, as well as across genres and styles. For instance, in primarily visual fiction, such as telecinematic fiction, performed theatre and graphic novels, the narrative events are partly represented through images. We see locations and events that take place in these locations, often without much need for verbal information. In contrast, many forms of written fiction lack images, which means that locations and events have to be represented through language. The same applies to characterisation. In visual forms of fiction, information such as the age and gender of characters is often established through images, which at times can even establish quite detailed and specific character information (Landert 2021b). In written fiction, characters are created entirely through language (see Section 5). Thus, the amount of descriptive language will typically vary across written fiction, performed fiction and telecinematic discourse.

In addition, language can be used in two different ways in fiction: the telling mode and the showing mode (Jahn 2021: 66; Rimmon-Kenan 2002: 110), and the distribution of these two modes varies across different types of fictional artefacts. The telling mode is typical of the narrative voice of overt narrators in written fiction, but it can also be found in the form of voice-over narrators in telecinematic fiction and in theatrical devices like the Greek chorus. In this mode, the narrator speaks to the audience, sometimes addressing the audience directly, sometimes just implying the audience as an addressee. In contrast, the showing mode is typically realised as character dialogue, where characters inside the fictional world talk to each other. This mode contributes most of the language in performed and telecinematic fiction, whereas its use in written fiction varies across literary genres. By observing character dialogues (for the functions of dialogue in fiction, see Bednarek 2017c, 2018: 33–77; Kozloff 2000; Locher & Jucker 2021: 128), the audience can see the narrative events unfold line by line. It is important to keep in mind that even though the audience is not the addressee of character dialogue, it is still its recipient. In other words, the character dialogue is designed for the benefit of the audience (see Leech & Short 2007: 242–245). Thus, dialogue in fiction always functions on two different levels simultaneously. On the one hand, it creates meaning within the fictional world, where fictional characters are assumed to interpret each other's lines. This is often referred to as the intradiegetic level of communication (Jucker & Locher 2017: 1). On the other hand, fictional dialogue creates meaning for the audience of the fictional artefact and, thus, is part of extradiegetic communication.

Both types of variation – the role of language for fiction and its mode – influence how the performance aspect of fiction is realised. For written fiction, one important aspect of performance is the presence of oral features (see Bublitz 2017). Linguistic features such as hesitations, fillers, false starts and overlaps, which are typical of spontaneous spoken interaction, are introduced into the written texts to create stylistic effects and to contribute to characterisation. In spoken forms of fiction – performed and telecinematic fiction – such oral features may, of course, perform similar functions, but they do not contribute to the performance aspect of language in the same way. Instead, the reduction of such oral features is one of the aspects that characterises dialogues in performed and telecinematic fiction in comparison to spontaneous spoken conversation. This is, at least in part, due to the fact that it is usually deemed important that the audience is able to understand the dialogue (for a discussion of a notable exception in the TV Series *The Wire* (2002–2008), see Toolan (2011)). For both written and spoken fiction, the degree to which stylised fictional dialogues integrate disfluencies of spontaneous conversations is a matter of style, which ranges from more realistic styles that are closer to spontaneous conversation to more theatrical styles with fewer disfluencies.

In the remainder of this section, we discuss the performance aspect of fiction from three perspectives. Section 3.2 will look at performance in written fiction, focusing in particular on the presentation of character talk and the presence of oral features. In Section 3.3, we will look at how utterances are carefully designed for maximum effect in performed fiction. Section 3.4 will discuss the role of the composition of multimodal cues for creating meaning in tele-cinematic fiction.

3.2 Written Fiction

Novels, short stories and poems regularly feature talking characters. It seems to be such a typical feature of written fiction that it is difficult to imagine fictional texts without the depiction of communication, sometimes in the form of thoughts of the narrator or a lyrical subject, but often in the form of spoken interactions between fictitious characters. Such conversations may be represented with the actual words spoken by the characters (as in Extract 3.1), they may be given in indirect speech (as in Extract 3.2), or they may be referred to in a more general way without reproducing the actual words spoken by the characters (as in Extract 3.3) (see Rimmon-Kenan 2002: 110–13; Semino & Short 2004; Vandelanotte 2009). The examples are all taken from the opening chapter of Sally Rooney's (2021) best-selling novel *Beautiful World, Where Are You*.

Extract 3.1 *Beautiful World, Where Are You* (Rooney 2021: location 89)

I'm so sorry about your mother, she said.
Yeah. Thanks.
I actually haven't seen my father in a while either. He's – not very reliable.
Felix looked up from his glass. Oh? he said. Drinker, is he?
Mm. And he— You know, he makes up stories.

Extract 3.2 *Beautiful World, Where Are You* (Rooney 2021: location 93)

He asked if she had siblings and she said one, a younger brother. He said he had a brother too.

Extract 3.3 *Beautiful World, Where Are You* (Rooney 2021: location 123)

For the rest of the walk to Alice's house, up along the coast road, they made conversation about Felix's social life, or rather Alice posed a number of queries on the subject which he mulled over and answered, both parties speaking more loudly than before due to the noise of the sea. He expressed no surprise at her questions, and answered them readily, but without speaking at excessive length or offering any information beyond what was directly solicited.

Extract 3.1 is an example of the showing mode. We are shown words that are exchanged between the two fictitious characters, but we are also given a bit of framing in the telling mode in the form of 'she said' appended to one of the utterances. Such additions help the readers to keep track of who said what in the exchange. Extract 3.2, which is an example of indirect speech representation, is a mixture of the showing and the telling mode. In Extract 3.3, the narrator describes how the two characters made conversation. Alice asked questions, and Felix answered them, but the actual words are not represented. This is a case of the telling mode. We are only told about the interaction.

In the showing mode, conversations in fictional texts sometimes create the impression of being very similar to unrehearsed spontaneous conversations in non-fictional contexts, but it is important to be aware of some basic differences between the two. In Extract 3.1, the two speakers use contractions (*I'm, haven't, he's*), hesitations (indicated by '—', i.e., em-dashes), discourse markers (*oh, you know*), a tag question (*is he?*) and an abbreviated response form (*mm*). We tend to associate these elements with oral production in unrehearsed everyday conversations, where speakers need to plan their utterances while they go along and also use them for stylistic or humorous purposes (Bublitz 2017; Jucker 2021; Locher & Jucker 2021: ch. 7). In fictional conversations as in Extract 3.1, for instance, such elements are not caused by the planning process; they are inserted for specific fictional and stylistic purposes. They show the speaker's hesitancy and unease in their first meeting.

Conversations in fictional texts can also be highly stylised, as, for instance, in Edgar Allan Poe's narrative poem 'The Raven', first published in 1845 (Poe 1967). The narrator remembers a dreary night in December when he was sitting by the fire, reading, and mourning the death of his beloved Lenore, when all of a sudden he perceives a tapping on the door. At first, the narrator suspects the arrival of an unexpected visitor, but then it turns out to be a raven knocking at the window. The poem consists of eighteen stanzas of six lines each with a complex rhythmical structure combined with end rhymes, internal rhymes and alliterations. About 40 per cent of the poem is given as direct speech. At the beginning, the narrator talks to himself when he hears a noise and assumes that an unexpected visitor must be calling: "''Tis some visiter,' I muttered, 'tapping at my chamber door – Only this and nothing more.'" In the fourth stanza, shown in Extract (3.4), he talks to the imagined visitor.

Extract 3.4 'The Raven' (Poe 1967: 77)

Presently my soul grew stronger; hesitating then no longer,
'Sir,' said I, 'or Madam, truly your forgiveness I implore;
But the fact is I was napping, and so gently you came rapping,

And so faintly you came tapping, tapping at my chamber door,
That I scarce was sure I heard you' – here I opened wide the door; –
                                   Darkness there and nothing more.

Once the raven has flown in through the window and perched itself on a bust over the door, the narrator addresses it in words of increasing urgency. He asks it for its name, its origin, and whether he will be able to forget his beloved Lenore, but the bird invariably replies with 'Nevermore'. Intermittently, the narrator also talks to himself again, musing about the bird's answer and its meanings. In the penultimate stanza of the poem, the narrator appears to be in a state of frenzy and charges the bird to leave him after it had, once again, only replied with 'Nevermore' (Extract 3.5).

Extract 3.5 'The Raven' (Poe 1967: 80)

'Be that word our sign of parting, bird or fiend!' I shrieked, upstarting –
'Get thee back into the tempest and the Night's Plutonian shore!
Leave no black plume as a token of that lie thy soul hath spoken!
Leave my loneliness unbroken! – quit the bust above my door!
Take thy beak from out my heart, and take thy form from off my door!'
                                 Quoth the Raven 'Nevermore.'

There are few, if any, prototypical features of orality in these lines, except perhaps for the repetitions and the frequent imperatives. The urgency of the words is conveyed through different means. In the showing mode, the author depicts the narrator's frantic address to 'bird or fiend' and his imploring words with a string of parallel imperatives. In the telling mode, the author uses the speech act verb 'shrieked' and describes how the narrator jumps up from his chair that earlier in the poem he had brought closer to the door so that he could more easily talk to the raven. It is clear that Poe does not attempt to provide a representation of spontaneous, everyday interaction. The narrator's utterances follow poetic demands rather than naturalistic ones.

A very different approach is taken by Douglas Adams in his mock science fiction novel *The Hitchhiker's Guide to the Galaxy* ([1979] 2005), in which the dialogues include many features of orality (see Jucker 2015), as for instance in Extract 3.6.

Extract 3.6 *The Hitchhiker's Guide to the Galaxy* (Adams [1979] 2005: 96)

'We've met,' said Arthur sharply.
[. . .]
'Er . . . what?' [Ford] said.
'I said we've met.'
Zaphod gave an awkward start of surprise and jabbed a gum sharply.
'Hey . . . er, have we? Hey . . . er . . . '

In this short extract, Zaphod is clearly taken by surprise by Arthur's announcement that he already knows the person to whom Ford has just tried to introduce him. This is shown through Zaphod's question ('have we?'), his uncertainty indicated by pauses with three dots (' ... '), the hesitator *er*, and the interjection *hey* and the unfinished construction at the end of the extract. The author clearly uses these features to characterise Zaphod's apprehension at this point. Zaphod is at a loss for words and does not know how to react. But it is important to realise that these features do not need to be a precise reflection of such features in a spontaneous conversation. They are carefully selected by the author to evoke a certain effect (see Bublitz 2017; Locher & Jucker 2021: 139–46).

It is possible that the high incidence of features of orality in the dialogues of this novel owes something to its origin as a radio play, but they are not produced because of a real need by the author of these lines (or the actor who utters them in a radio play) to think about what to say next. They are produced to suggest – in a stylised way – such hesitation and uncertainty on the part of the fictitious character. In the next section, we turn to such processes in performed fiction.

3.3 Performed Fiction

Scripted and rehearsed theatre shares many similarities with written fiction when it comes to the deliberate placement of orality features. The actors of rehearsed plays know their lines well and the turn-taking has usually been decided long before the performance. Apart from interventions by the audience (see Section 4.3) and accidental departures from the rehearsed script, there is no need for actors to repair their utterances, ask for clarifications or bridge silences to search for words, while all these tasks have to be managed locally and ad hoc by interactants in spontaneous conversations. This means that the features of orality are, at least for the most part, intentionally placed for their dramatic effect, much like in written and telecinematic fiction.

So far, the use of orality features in theatrical performances has received very little attention in linguistics. An important exception is Norrthon's (2019) study of the performance of overlap in the Riksteatren's production of Lucy Prebble's play *The Effect*. Norrthon traces the performance of a short passage from the play across the entire production process, from the first rehearsal where the actors read the script together for the first time to the performance on the opening night. His analysis is based on video recordings of the rehearsals and performances, which also give him access to rehearsal talk and instructions by the director relating to the scene. The passage includes an overlap that is indicated in the script by the playwright and Norrthon shows how closely the actors orient towards the playwright in their first reading by producing the overlap exactly as indicated in the script. In subsequent rehearsals, the role of the overlap is discussed and emphasised by the actors and the director, resulting in more and longer overlaps. In contrast, by the opening night the overlap is once again reduced, but the wording has undergone certain changes, due to small improvisations. Thus, the final form of delivery on the opening night is the result of a collaborative rehearsal process involving the script, the actors and the director. Norrthon does not investigate whether and how the production of the overlap changes over the course of the performances, but it is possible that audience responses during the performance can influence subsequent productions of the overlap even further (see also Section 4.3). Norrthon's study shows that orality features like overlaps are carefully designed for maximum effect in scripted and rehearsed theatre.

In improvised theatre, there are two different sources of orality features. Like in scripted plays, orality features can be deliberately placed for dramatic effect. In addition, the online production process can result in hesitations, self-corrections and overlaps that are due to online planning problems and floor negotiation. In general, it is not possible for the audience – or for the researcher – to decide whether a certain instance of such a feature is deliberate or not. However, there are passages for which it is plausible to assume that they resulted from communication problems between the two performers. An example of this are requests for clarification, as in Extract 3.7, by the improvisation duo TJ & Dave.

Extract 3.7 *TJ & Dave – Blurting in Earnest* (2016, 00:43:01–00:43:05)

Dave: Do you want anything?
TJ: What's that?
Dave: Do you want anything?
TJ: No I'm doing real good.

In this passage, TJ responds to Dave's question with 'What's that?', causing Dave to repeat his question. While it is impossible to know what the performer's reason was for producing this question, it seems plausible that it was caused by his failure to understand his partner's utterance. In the entire performance of roughly one hour, there are fourteen instances of 'What's that?', all of which are used in a similar way, and the same pattern can also be observed in other performances by TJ & Dave, which suggests that this is one of the ways in which these two performers deal with auditory problems. A closer look at such passages might provide further information on how improvisers deal with such small communication problems during their performance.

Apart from orality features, there are a range of other features that are characteristic of language performed for an audience. Like in written fiction, these include poetic language use, rhymes and alliterations, puns and other types of verbal humour, as well as the use of repetition and the creation of patterns in communication, such as specific sequences of turns (see the use of *metaphorically (speaking)* after suggestions in Extract 3.8). A short passage from the improvised performance of *Ella & Stacey – Close Quarters: Cruise Ship* (2021b) can illustrate some of these features. The events in this performance take place on a present-day cruise ship and they feature several guests and members of staff. All characters are performed by the two improvisers, Ella Galt and Stacey Smith. One of these characters is a sailor, Jeremy, who is portrayed in the style of a pirate. He speaks with a stylised accent that is often used in the portrayal of pirates in telecinematic discourse. He makes frequent use of archaic language (e.g., *ye* for *you*) and colourful verbal imagery, as in Extract 3.8, where he provides relationship advice to the captain of the ship.

Extract 3.8 *Ella & Stacey – Close Quarters: Cruise Ship* (2021b, 00:14:04–00:16:18)

```
1   Jeremy:  I suggest we throw her overboard. (to Captain, who looks
2            shocked) Metaphorically, from your heart. Cast her out, cast
3            her aside, make her walk the plank of your emotional wrath, Sir.
4            Sir.
5   [...]
6   Jeremy:  [...] and if this woman doesn't recognise the value in you, we
7            toss her to the sharks. Metaphorically speaking.
8            [...]
9            we- we- we- we- we tie her up and sink her to the bottom of
10           the ocean. Metaphorically.
11           [...]
12  Jeremy:  We- we Jolly Roger her by the rails.
```

In this passage, there are various references to pirate themes, such as letting someone 'walk the plank' (line 3) and feeding them to the sharks (line 7), as well as a reference to the pirate flag, known as Jolly Roger (line 12). These references are used in metaphors, in which killing someone (in a pirate way) stands for ending one's romantic involvement with the person. The captain is shocked about Jeremy's suggestions (line 1), leading Jeremy to point out repeatedly that they are only meant metaphorically (lines 2, 7, 10), a statement that is echoed twice in later parts of the performance by different characters.

One of the performance aspects of language in theatre is that it allows performers to demonstrate their skills with respect to the delivery and, in the case of improvised theatre, the creation of well-composed dialogue. In Extract 3.8, the audience can admire the performer's ability to come up with several pirate-themed metaphors for ending a relationship. In another type of improvised performance, *Hitch*Cocktails* (2021) – an improvised thriller in the style of Alfred Hitchcock – the quick-wittedness of the improvisers is given centre stage at different moments during the play. At the beginning of the play, the six improvisers ask the audience to share a personal fear, which they use as an inspiration for locations, characters, plot and even verbal humour throughout their performance. Extract 3.9 is from the beginning of the play. The performers received the suggestion 'goldfish' from the audience and they use this as inspiration for coming up with a title and a tagline, with as little as forty seconds to think about this and without discussion among themselves, while Player 1 explains certain aspects of the upcoming show to the audience.

> Extract 3.9 *Hitch*Cocktails* (2021)
>
> Player 1: And now, without further ado, Hitch*Cocktails is proud to present
> to you the thriller entitled
> Player 2: Fins Up
> Player 1: With the exciting tag line that reads
> Player 3: It's sink or swim when a pet shop owner becomes embroiled in
> a perfect murder plot. Will they be able to get out through the
> scales of justice? Or become green in the gills.

The title and especially the tagline provide the performers with points of orientation for the plot – for instance, the first scene of the play shows a pet shop owner – while at the same time they entertain and impress the audience through wordplay related to the suggestion 'goldfish'.

In performed fiction, actors perform live in front of an audience who came to see a play expecting to be entertained, emotionally moved and/or aesthetically pleased and who, in most cases, even paid a fee to see the performance. It is plausible that the knowledge that such an audience is present affects the way in which language is used on stage, but how exactly this is the case has hardly been studied yet. The same is true for the effect of audience interaction during the performance, which we will discuss in Section 4.3.

3.4 Telecinematic Fiction

We have previously referred to performance in telecinematic discourse as 'frozen' and we will use this section to address that attribute and telecinematic performance more generally. Reducing fiction to the most prototypical examples, written, performed and telecinematic fiction share that the written text that constitutes them or on which they are based is frozen: once published, additional voices may be added to the paratext (Section 2.2), but the text itself is printed and final. In written fiction, this is apparent because the text itself is what readers engage with; in non-improvised theatre, the text may also be available as a printed book and therefore exists in a fixed and published form (although performances may of course alter the wording of the text in spoken perform-ance); in telecinematic fiction, the screenplay may not be commonly read as fiction, but it too is final. When it comes to performance, however, the three types of fiction are clearly distinct in that in written fiction intradiegetic actions are always represented rather than enacted (but see Section 3.2 for different degrees of showing and telling), performed fiction dynamically stages fiction for each of its unique performances (Section 3.3) and telecinematic fiction presents a performance to its viewers that remains the same in each screening and is thus frozen. Put differently, the defining text that constitutes a telecinematic artefact is not the written text of the screenplay, but its frozen multimodal performance.

While it is thus accurate in a broad sense to conceive of telecinematic performance as frozen, it is important to also take into account the dynamic aspects of its production and reception. To begin with, we have highlighted in Section 2.4 that communication through fictional film and television consists of many different processes, and the performance can only be thought of as unchanged over time when we limit the pragmatics of telecinematic fiction to reception of the final product, excluding the multiple performances that took place during its production. However, even if we disregard the processes that shape language use in and of film, we still need to acknowledge that viewing film and television is itself a situated practice, influenced by the setting in which it takes place (see Section 4.4). When looking more closely at film reception, it becomes clear that viewers of telecinematic fiction in fact engage with a performance (screening) of a performance (artefact).[3] Both types of performance are of interest to pragmatic scholarship in terms of the particular communicative practices they give rise to, and regarding the multimodal context in which language is embedded. In this section, we will deal with the performance in the artefact and in Section 4.4 we will return to screening differences.

---

[3] To complicate matters further, the performance frozen in the artefact may in fact not be one monolithic performance but a group of similar performances adapted for different viewings. Examples are remastered or restored versions of films, reformatted editions for television or in-flight entertainment and, most obviously, translations into other languages.

In the domain of the performance frozen in the artefact, the meaning of a fictional telecinematic artefact is based on a complex arrangement of different semiotic modes. In Figure 1 and in Section 2.4, we have highlighted some of the participants whose creative work is encoded in the final multimodal text, and we will reiterate here some of the most relevant modes that contribute to the artefact and thus also to the language of fictional film and television.

Broadly, performance in this sense consists of the work of the cast and crew and thus of *acting* and *staging*. Acting here refers to the embodied performance by actors playing fictional characters, a crucial element of which is typically spoken dialogue. As is the case for stage actors' performances (Section 3.3), actors' language use is informed by a range of situational properties. These include conventions of telecinematic storytelling, the specific story and plot of the artefact, characterisation (Section 5), the interaction with other characters, the persona of the actor (Section 5.3), the writing style of the scriptwriters, the commercial aim of the producers, assumptions about the target audience, and so on. Moreover, spoken telecinematic dialogue, much like face-to-face dialogue, is accompanied by facial expressions, gestures and other paralinguistic and non-linguistic actions insofar as they are understood as communicatively meaningful by viewers. Since context is essential to meaning-making, the embodied paralinguistic context of the actor's performance and the larger fictional and non-fictional contexts of the actor–characters' interactions are both essential components for understanding what and how telecinematic artefacts create meaning.

It is important to note, too, that telecinematic fiction is not mediated automatically. Leaving aside the philosophical debate over whether or not photographic images themselves are objective and automatic (as claimed by Bazin ([1958] 1960) and refuted by Carroll (1988: 153–7), see also Brubaker's (1993) discussion), staging for telecinematic fiction is an intentional meaning-making process that does not simply reproduce actors' performances as they would have been seen by those present during filming. Instead, cinematic storytelling is a multimodal enterprise that is shaped by patterns and conventions – a 'grammar' of film, which creates meaning beyond what the moving images represent. We leave it to film and cinema studies to discuss in detail every audiovisual aspect this entails (for a good overview see Bordwell et al. (2020)), but it is important for scholars in pragmatics, too, to take into account the way in which make-up and costumes, set design and lighting, sound and music, camera angles and movements, etc., together with character dialogue, form a multimodal composite signal. The linguistic cues are thus situated within a multimodal context.

The interaction of modes characteristic of telecinematic fiction can be illustrated nicely with the help of Extract 3.10, from *Groundhog Day*.

Extract 3.10 *Groundhog Day* (1993: 00:21:08–00:21:15)

Phil Connors is standing on the doorstep of his hotel. People are all walking in the same direction. Phil starts talking to a woman who turns around and responds to his question.

Phil: excuse me– excuse me, where's everybody going?
Woman: to Gobbler's Knob. it's Groundhog Day.

In order to discuss the meaning of these two utterances in the film, we will start from the lines of dialogue and then add layers of multimodal context. At the text surface, one character, Phil, asks another character a question, a request for information, and receives an answer, a relevant explanation of where everyone is going. In addition, the woman specifies what day it is, Groundhog Day, which indicates that she is surprised Phil does not know the answer to his question. Viewers of the film, in contrast, will have a very clear understanding of what is going on, because by this time in the film they have already received a wealth of information to contextualise the interaction. They have seen how Phil, a weather man travelling to Punxsutawney to report on the yearly Groundhog Day, has gone to the festivities in the town centre, commented on the groundhog seeing a shadow, and fallen asleep in his hotel room the evening before. Now, just before he left the hotel, viewers have heard the radio alarm clock turn on to play the same song as the day before, then the same radio hosts talking about the weather and Groundhog Day, repeating verbatim what they had said just a bit earlier in the film. A specific film sound,[4] a chime with rising frequency, has indicated that something strange is going on. The sound has accompanied, for instance, Phil's encounter with a man in the hotel corridor who repeats exactly what he said the previous day, and it was audible again right before Phil starts addressing the passer-by. In short, the viewers have begun to understand that Phil is caught in a time loop, reliving the same day over and over.

When he asks where everyone is going, the answer is both obvious, because it is Groundhog Day and everyone is on their way to the festivities at Gobbler's Knob, and confusing, as for Phil it could not be Groundhog Day, since this day – for him – already happened the day before. The clash between the two interpretations, represented by the two characters in Extract 3.10, could easily be rendered in written fiction as well. However, the way in which recipients arrive

---

[4] Flückiger (2001) calls sounds like this one *unidentifizierte Klangobjekte* ('unidentified sound objects'), referring to sounds for which viewers cannot infer a source inside the story world.

at the understanding of bewilderment at the events, surprise at the question, and their overall significance for the story, is characteristic for telecinematic fiction. The composite signal of film fuses the subjective perspective of the main character and the intersubjective experiences of all other characters into one diegetic reality, while using sounds, music, images and dialogue not only to show a complex story world but also to tell a multimodal story to viewers.

When considering the type of cues included in the composite signal, it is worth pointing out that what characters in these stories do is also influenced by events and developments in the real world. For example, many films in the 1980s and 1990s have represented computer- and internet-based practices such as writing on a keyboard, surfing the internet or hacking in ways that have given rise to new cinematic conventions. For instance, notification sounds for incoming email and graphic representations of the progress of hacking (e.g., *Sneakers* (1992)) have been included in film. More recently, the pervasiveness of communication via mobile phones has meant that text-based messaging has appeared in films and television series in various forms – from showing phone screens in close-up (e.g., *Scott Pilgrim vs. the World* (2010)) to various types of pop-ups appearing next to the character, superimposed on the film image (e.g., *Sherlock* (2010)). Just as there are epistolary novels that incorporate letter-writing into fiction, films also find ways not just to tell their viewers about new communicative practices but also to develop a visual language of representing them. One effect of this may be that spoken dialogue as the dominant mode of language in film is starting to share the spotlight with more and more writing on the screen. As we will show in Section 4.4, new community-based practices, such as viewer comments, contribute to this development.

3.5 Summary

Irrespective of whether they are written or performed, spontaneously produced or scripted, delivered to audiences live or as frozen recordings, all fictional artefacts are designed and put on display for an audience. As we have shown in this section, this leads to rich and complex texts in which different modes of expression are combined in meaningful ways. Oral features are carefully staged in written and performed texts, and image, sound and language are combined into complex multimodal artefacts in which each mode adds an additional layer of meaning. In addition, fictional artefacts put the skills of text producers on display through the use of poetic language, clever multimodal compositions, authentic and expressive performances by actors and the quick-wittedness of improvisers.

Many of these aspects have received only very little attention by linguists so far, despite the fact that the display and foregrounding of form–function–meaning relationships (this is Bauman's (2000: 1) definition of performance) provide excellent opportunities for pragmatic studies. One type of fictional artefact which is especially underexplored is performed fiction, which has often been studied only on the basis of play texts, rather than performances. Another huge topic which we could only touch upon in this section is the process that leads up to the performance, for example the rehearsal process of scripted theatre and the editing of written and telecinematic fiction. By studying this process from a pragmatic perspective, one could explore in much more depth what choices text producers make in composing their artefact for an audience.

4 Interaction

4.1 Introducing Research Avenues into Interaction with Fiction

Traditionally, the communicative setting of engagement with fictional texts is understood to be separable along the production–reception axis into stages, as well as participant roles (but see Section 2 for the complexity of the participation structure in fiction). A very simple model of fictional texts discerns a production stage, in which fictional texts are told, written, staged and filmed, and a reception stage, in which listening, reading and viewing happen. On the level of participation, individuals and groups are either senders of fictional messages, or they are recipients, and thus readers, audiences, viewers. It is evident that even in the most traditional and prototypical setting, the clear separation of these stages is a model rather than a realistic representation of production and reception processes: authors may, for instance, read their own books, and playwrights and filmmakers may stage their own plays or direct their own films, or perhaps even act in them or sit in the audience while what they have authored is performed by someone else. What we address in this section, however, is that the convergence of roles – apparent in concepts such as wreader (writing reader, e.g., Kouta 2021; Landow 2006), prosumer (a blend of producer and consumer, e.g., Olin-Scheller & Wikström 2010) or participatory audience (e.g., Reason 2015; Schlütz & Jage-D'Aprile 2021) – is less and less an exception that warrants only a footnote. Instead, it has become a possibility for many who engage with fiction to also contribute to its production, and a defining characteristic for some genres of fiction is that they are co-produced by the community for which they are made.

One pragmatic effect of the temporal and spatial distance that exists between makers and recipients in traditional written and telecinematic fiction is the lack of grounding (Clark & Brennan 1991; Clark & Schaefer 1987). Those who communicate have no way of knowing whether what they intended matches what those who listen understand, and accordingly they design the fictional text in particular ways. The interaction between authors and audiences, or lack thereof, is bound to have far-reaching effects on the shape and form of a fictional artefact, including its mimetic and diegetic use of language. In some cases, literary texts may be purposefully open to many interpretations, as Barthes (1970) indicated with his concept of the *scriptable* ('writerly') text. In other cases, telecinematic texts may employ redundancies across semiotic modes and repetitions to make texts more *lisible* ('readerly') and reduce the effort that is necessary to understand them.

One interesting aspect in artefact–recipient interaction is control over the reception process: readers of traditional novels have no say in what is written in the novel, but they are free to skip or re-read passages. Audiences of performed fiction, on the other hand, have no such options concerning reception and time, but they can share evaluative and other responses through applause or by shouting towards the stage. Reception of telecinematic fiction, finally, is characterised by very different ways of engagement: in the movie theatre, the linear telling of the story is as much out of the viewers' control as it is in a theatre. In contrast, on a personal device, a computer or a mobile phone, the recipient's control over their viewing resembles that of the novel reader. In both cases, however, viewer response will remain unheard by anyone involved in the making of the telecinematic artefact.

Outside of the most typical reception settings, more interactive modes have existed for a long time. Audiences of test-screenings see films before they are released, and their responses may influence the final shape of the film itself (see, e.g., Weaving et al. 2018) or the framing of its distribution and thus the context in which it is received; different stages of fictional writing may take place interactively, for instance in writing groups or in a classroom setting (e.g., McDonough et al. 2021); and audience contributions are often an integral part of improvisation theatre.

More recent developments in terms of technologies and habits of engagement with fictional texts have meant that the role of recipients in meaning-making has expanded. The literature on the pragmatics of social media has explored some of the stories – fictional and non-fictional – that are told by non-professional members of a community to the community. For example, on streaming platforms such as Viki.com, viewers are also writers of subtitles and contributors of comments, both of which are distributed together with streamed television episodes. Professionally produced artefacts are transformed and adapted into new artefacts when film stills are made into memes to be shared on social media, or when lay or expert viewership of fictional films is given centre stage in new derivative videos. For instance, experts in a particular field may comment on fictional scenes from movies that contain their area of expertise (e.g., shooting arrows, being a bodyguard, climbing). Readers of e-books can not only highlight and comment on passages in their reading like readers of print books, but they can also share their contributions with other readers.

Some of these new modes of reader and viewer participation influence subsequent artefacts (sequels, episodes, performances), while others change the very artefact they orient towards. In either case, they affect the boundaries between text and other texts, between text and paratext and between different types of participants engaged in communication in and through fiction. That development, from text to hypertext, from reader to wreader, from consumer to prosumer, also demands a new form of scholarship that understands the fictional text as a more dynamic and collaborative construct that keeps being expanded and enriched with new voices. In what follows, we will build up this argument by first focusing on the interaction between author and text (Section 4.2), then the interaction between audience and performers (Section 4.3), and we will end with a discussion of the interaction between the audience and the telecinematic artefact as 'product' (Section 4.4).

4.2 Written Fiction

Most forms of written communication, whether fictional or not, are instances of asynchronous communication – the time of writing the text and the time of reading it are set apart. In some cases, the time lag may be very short, as when somebody jots a few words on a piece of paper and pushes it over to a recipient, who picks it up and immediately reads it, or when we exchange electronic messages in quick succession via computers or mobile phones. However, the time lag may extend over many centuries, as for instance when we read a novel by Charles Dickens (1812–70), Jane Austen (1775–1817) or Daniel Defoe (c. 1660–1731), or even further back when we read a text that was originally written in the Middle Ages, e.g., the Old English poem 'Beowulf' or the writings of Geoffrey Chaucer (c. 1342/3–1400). In such cases, it seems natural to think in terms of one-way communication. The author, who lived a long time ago, wrote a book that we read today, and there is no way in which we can talk back to the author. However, the communicative situation is more complex. The fictional artefact is not a static entity, but essentially dynamic. As we argued in Section 2, the fictional text is embedded within a paratext (Genette 1997), which includes the book cover with the title of the book, the name of the author, artwork and endorsements, as well as a wider context of recommendations, reviews and so on.

And even the text itself is typically modified, in some cases very significantly, from the version written by the author to the version read by the reader. Even in the most straightforward cases in which authors write their own text on a computer, the text is likely to undergo some minor, or less minor, modifications to the layout, pagination, font choices and so on before it ends up in the hands of the reader. The text may have been desk edited by the publisher, and in the case of older texts, this editing may be quite extensive. When we read Jane Austen's *Pride and Prejudice* (1813), for instance, we read a text that was originally handwritten before it was turned into print, and typically we do not read a first-edition copy, but an edited version in which the text is surrounded by an introduction, a description of the textual history, explanatory notes and perhaps a list of textual emendations.

For medieval texts, the necessary mediation is even more extensive. Let us take Chaucer's *Canterbury Tales* (1987) as an example. They were written at the end of the fourteenth century in what is now called Middle English, a version of English that is not easily understandable for a present-day audience. The tales have survived in a large number of almost contemporary handwritten manuscripts, but none in Chaucer's own hand. What we read today when we read these tales is, therefore, heavily mediated. It is based on the work of generations of specialists who used the various sources to establish different versions of the text. Such versions of the text include scholarly editions, which try to create a text that is as close as possible to what might have been the original text. They add not only footnotes, textual glosses, notes on alternative readings in different manuscripts, glossaries and so on, but they typically also impose a layout that is easier to read for a modern audience, and they generally add punctuation and substitute some obsolete characters by modern ones. These editions, in an act of mediation, try to give students of Middle English a tool to get as close as possible to the original text written by Chaucer, but in a crucial sense they do not produce the original text itself.

Other editions deviate even more from the original. They modernise the text into present-day English, or they translate the text into a different language. Such modernisations and translations sometimes retain – or rather try to re-create – the poetic composition of the original, with its complex structure of rhyme and rhythm; or they prefer a prose rendering, which often makes it easier to capture subtle shades of meaning but which introduces other deviations from the original.

However, the process of mediation, which necessarily stands between the writing and the reading of written fiction, is only one part of its dynamic nature, because a fictional text never exists without precursors (for the concept of intertextuality, see Kristeva 1980 [1977]). Chaucer's *Canterbury Tales* may again serve as an example. Many of the texts are based on earlier narratives. Chaucer often translated texts that he was familiar with either from Latin or from Old French. He never did this without very creatively reworking the material that he used as an inspiration for his own work. And needless to say, his writings have inspired generations of other writers over the last 600 years. Thus, we can visualise written fiction as a process of mediation and inspiration as depicted in Figure 2.

Figure 2 depicts the process by which a piece of written fiction is mediated into many different readings, and how such readings may be the inspirations for new texts. Such inspirations can take many different forms. We have mentioned some textual influences that Chaucer used when he wrote his *Canterbury Tales*, and it seems difficult to imagine any piece of fiction that has not been influenced or inspired by the personal reading experiences of the author. Such influences may be very fleeting in the form of genre expectations, literary motives, topics or some incidental details, but they may also be more tangible. In the case of serial writing, individual episodes may be directly influenced by the reactions of readers of earlier ones (see Section 5.4 on the serial writing of Charles Dickens). Some works of fiction are explicitly written as spin-offs of other works of fiction; that is to say, they are based on another piece of fiction and develop some of the characters, events or other aspects of

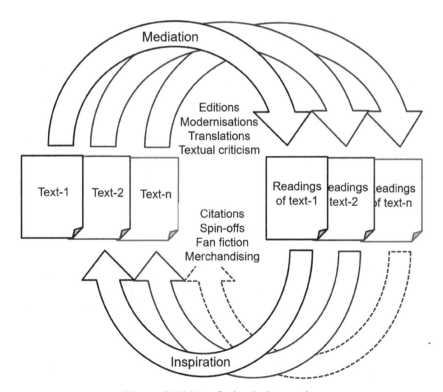

Figure 2 Written fiction in interaction

the story world in a new context (Locher & Jucker 2021: 254). This may take the form of a prequel or sequel in which the new context is situated in a temporal context before or after the original time frame respectively, or the texts can play at the same time but, for example, explore the events through the perspective of a different character.

In Figure 2, the written text is seen as a starting point which is embedded in paratexts and mediated in possibly multifarious ways to the reading public, and it is seen as the result of inspirations by the author's manifold reading experiences. In Sections 4.3 and 4.4, we will explore the interaction layers when written texts (e.g., a play, or a movie script) are staged and turned into multimodal performed artefacts.

4.3 Performed Fiction

In contrast to written and telecinematic fiction, theatrical fiction is performed in the presence of a live audience. This means that the performers receive feedback from the audience on how the performance is received, for instance through applause, laughter, emotional gasps or even verbal contributions. In addition to affecting the viewing experience of other audience members (see also Section 4.4), such feedback can affect the performance and even the content of a fictional artefact. In this section, we are taking a closer look at the different forms the participation of the audience can take and at how these influence fictional artefacts.

Theatre and performance studies have investigated the role of the audience in the performance from a theoretical perspective. Fischer-Lichte (2008: 163) has coined the term 'autopoetic feedback loop' to refer to the 'mutual interaction between actors and spectators [that] brings forth the performance'. In her understanding, the audience is always an active participant in the interaction with performers. Spectators are emotionally and even bodily affected by the performance, which creates a circulation of energy that influences the actors and the overall performance. According to Fischer-Lichte, this is even the case when there is no audible verbal contribution or active intervention by the audience. One of the consequences of this is that each performance is 'unique and unrepeatable' (2008: 51), since the presence of the audience will lead to slightly different realisations of plays each time they are performed.

The way in which the presence of the audience affects fictional artefacts has hardly been studied from a linguistic perspective. As mentioned in earlier chapters, the vast majority of linguistic research on theatre has focused on the study of play texts rather than performances. An exception is Broth (2011), who studies audience laughter and vocal noises in five play performances in French. As far as laughter is concerned, he finds that audiences tend to laugh as a group in coordination with each other, rather than individually. His findings also indicate that audience members often hold their laughter until the next transition relevance place in the dialogue, which he interprets as an attempt to maintain understandability of the performed dialogue. With respect to the effect of the audience laughter on the play, his findings show that the actors also take the audience laughter into account by delaying their next turns, while non-verbal communication such as nodding continues.

The conventions concerning the amount and form of audience feedback that is expected or tolerated vary a great deal across types of performances, venues, style and genre, and they also change over time. In present-day highbrow theatre, the audience is often expected to remain quiet throughout a performance and – apart from an appropriate amount of laughter in the right places – restrict feedback to applause at the end of a play and possibly between acts. This is rather different from what we know about audience behaviour in eighteenth-century theatres in London, described by Fisher (2003) as follows:

> The town's displeasure with a manager's decision, or a dramatist's script, or a player's performance or nonappearance, could result in varying degrees of disruptive behavior, from full-scale rioting and pelting the stage with fruit and other objects to hissing players and demanding apologies. The theatre-goers' pleasure could be equally disruptive; they might call for several encores of a particular speech or song, or cheer so loudly that, even if a performance were not brought to a halt, the actors could not be heard. (Fisher 2003: 56)

Fisher goes on to explain that such audience interventions could, for instance, lead to changes in the script of subsequent performances and the replacement of cast members even within an ongoing performance.

While this is no longer the expected behaviour of audiences in most theatres, there are still contexts in which the audience is granted a more active role in more recent periods. An example is Augusto Boal's Theatre of the Oppressed, where audience involvement and participation form part of the endeavour of making theatre address political issues. In this style of theatre, the audience may be asked to comment on the portrayal of events on stage, or even be invited to join the performance. Other popular examples of invited audience participation can be found in Christmas pantomimes, and shows such as the Rocky Horror Show, where audience participation at specific points of the production and in well-defined forms has become scripted into the show to such an extent that theatres and screening venues might even hand out props to the audience before the show.

In improvised theatre, audience interaction is the norm rather than the exception. The audience is often asked for suggestions either at the beginning of a performance or even throughout, depending on the form and style of the improvisation.

Also, the type of contribution the audience is invited to make varies (see Lösel 2013: 159–85). In what follows, a few examples will illustrate the range of forms audience contributions can take in improvised theatre.

Many performances start with improvisers asking the audience for a suggestion to start the show (see also Extract (3.9) in Section 3), this can be a single word (4.1), a phrase (4.2), a location (4.3), or something more specific, like a personal fear or a secret.

> Extract 4.1 *Devil's Daughter* (2021), 3 November
>
> Elicitation: 'All we need from you to get us started is a suggestion of something that is not a food'
> Suggestion: 'Mallet'
>
> Extract 4.2 *Super Human* (2021), 27 October
>
> Elicitation: 'Can I have a suggestion of something that someone actually said to you today?'
> Suggestion: 'Why do people give you so much feedback?'
>
> Extract 4.3 *Ella & Stacey – Close Quarters: Church* (2021a), 14 August
>
> Elicitation: '[. . .] a place that this performance can take place in'
> Suggestion: 'A church'

The way in which these suggestions influence the performance varies a great deal. The suggestion in Extract (4.2) led to a beginning of a first scene in which feedback played an important role and from which a coherent narrative was further developed. The word in Extract (4.1) was explored for its various associations in a rather abstract opening scene. These different associations of *mallet* then inspired a number of subsequent scenes that were not integrated into an overall single narrative. In Extract (4.3), the suggestion *church* was used as a place in which the entire show was set. While some scenes took place inside a church, others dealt with the community that was organised around the church and church events. Characters were recurring and the scenes were connected in multiple ways, for example through reference to common characters and events.

Audience suggestions can also be used to inspire characters. For instance, in *Family Dinner* (2021), each performer receives a secret from the audience that will be the secret of the fictional character throughout the improvised two-act play. Yet another option is to ask a member of the audience for a real-life event that has recently happened (*Fuck This Week* 2021) or that is about to take place (*Middleditch & Schwartz: Parking Lot Wedding* 2020). The performers then engage in an extended conversation with the audience member, eliciting further details about the event and the various individuals

involved in it, which provide rich inspirations for the subsequent performance. In addition to suggestions at the beginning of a show, the audience can
also be asked for input during the performance, for instance when they are
asked to decide which of various story beginnings should be continued
(*Super Scene* 2021).

The amount of audience intervention in improvised theatre varies greatly. At
the less interactive end of the scale are performances like *TJ & Dave: Blurting
in Earnest* (2016), in which the two performers start their show without inviting
any audience suggestions at all. Still, the audience can influence the show in
ways that affect further events, for instance by alerting the performers to the
humorous potential of certain aspects of their performance, of which they may
not have been aware themselves (see Landert 2021a: 78).

At the opposite end of the scale are performances like *MOLLY* (2021), in
which audience members join the performance. In this particular instance, the
involvement of the audience member was not planned by the performers, as an
after-show interview with the performers and the audience member confirmed. In their show, the two improvisers regularly address the audience or
individual members of the audience as if they were part of the fictional world.
They may ask an audience member for a specific piece of information, such as
their name, but they do not expect the audience to interact with them more
extensively. In this scene, the performers are playing a couple who are waiting
for a woman whom they want to interview as a potential surrogate mother for
their child. They address a member of the audience as the candidate and this
audience member, who happens to have experience in improvised theatre,
decides to get up, enter the stage and join the scene as the interviewee. Thus,
she changes her role from a member of an audience to a performer and later
back to an audience member.

As the examples in this section have shown, there is a wide variety of ways in
which the audience of performed fiction can interact with the performers and the
fictional artefact. Most of these forms have not been studied yet from a linguistic
perspective, and there are a great deal of open questions for research, such as the
way in which non-verbal audience response like laughter influences the production of fictional dialogue by the performers, and how improvisers adopt,
adjust and build on verbal contributions by the audience.

4.4 Telecinematic Fiction

In Section 3.4, we explored the metaphor of the 'frozen' artefact to speak of the
multimodal performance that can be enjoyed repeatedly. In the case of
a 'frozen' artefact, and in contrast to live theatre performances, immediate

interaction with the actors and influencing the artefact in ways that directly change its form and dynamics are not possible. However, we made the case that it is important to reflect on how reception and pragmatic meaning-making processes change depending on how this watching takes place, i.e., on how the viewers interact with the artefact. In this section, we explore these ideas further by focusing on the factors that influence interpretation and the different interaction possibilities with the artefact itself, which, as we will argue below, may nevertheless change the artefact in certain contexts.

In previous sections, we discussed how the paratext of a fictional artefact influences how it is interpreted. There are movie and TV series trailers, and posters advertising the product, through which the collective producers entice us to watch. The use of genre labels such as sitcom, drama, thriller, etc. guide viewer expectations. There might be printed or performed precursors in the form of books, webtoons and theatre productions that influence our viewing. In fact, there is also a plethora of texts that is produced by the audience itself that has the potential to influence the viewers. Reading texts that provide critical engagement with the artefact, such as professional and lay reviews, scholarly interpretations, viewer ratings, etc., will impact viewers' decisions to watch, as well as their actual viewing experience. Both the professional and the lay comments can thus shape the interpretation of the artefact.

Next to these texts that allow for a dense network of potential influencing input, we also need to peruse the actual viewing context further. As mentioned before, the term 'telecinematic' encompasses both artefacts that are produced for the small screen (e.g., the television in the living room) and for the cinema (Piazza et al. 2011). The distinction between these two contexts has always been blurry as movies for the cinema eventually make it to the small screen, and it has become even harder to maintain now that new release patterns have been adopted and artefacts are more often released via different outlets at the same time. In addition, the ways in which telecinematic artefacts can be consumed have multiplied in recent years. Viewers can watch on their smartphone, tablet, laptop, desktop, TV screen, airplane monitor, on their own or in groups, in a private space such as their home or more public spaces like pubs and restaurants, or at watch parties online. Movies can be consumed in all of the contexts just described but also in a cinema theatre, IMAX theatre or in an open-air cinema, or can be projected on the wall of viewers' local movie club. In each scenario, the here and now will affect how viewers watch, experience and interpret the artefact.

When viewers watch on their own, their viewing experience will differ from when they watch with others because when watching together viewers co-construct meaning in a more collaborative way. When they watch in the same space, they have access to the immediate reactions of their fellow viewers, like in a theatre performance. For example, they might share emotional reactions to a humorous or scary scene. This will then reinforce their own interpretation. If they do not share the emotional reactions, they might wonder about the other's perception and learn about their reaction and interpretation. Depending on the frame expectations for the viewing context, viewers might discuss issues of plot or actor performance (e.g., at home) or they might refrain from voicing their ideas aloud (e.g., in the movie theatre). Once they hear someone else's reaction and interpretation, their own take on what they see will be influenced.

Co-presence of viewing does not have to take place in the same physical space. Computer-mediated communication affordances make it possible to combine different communication channels and to watch at the same time in different locations. Streaming platforms such as Disney+, Netflix or Viki provide affordances to watch at the same time in so-called watch parties. Watching together online can also be organised more informally so that viewers combine different programmes and affordances. For example, they might watch on a streaming platform or at home in front of their TV at the same time, but use Twitter, Discord or Reddit threads to react to and discuss what they see. This has been discussed as second screen practices in the literature (e.g., Androutsopoulos & Weidenhöffer 2015; Schirra et al. 2014). Some streaming platforms, such as Bilibili, allow the placing of comments on the display of the streamed video, so-called danmaku, that will provide a reaction to and interpretation of what happens on screen by viewers (e.g., Zhang & Cassany 2019a, 2019b). Since these danmaku can clutter the screen when many viewers interact, the viewing experience of the original artefact is changed.

A particular case of co-viewing is provided on the streaming platform Viki, which achieves an effect of seeming co-presence by presenting temporally distant comments as a seamless sequence of utterances: the platform allows viewers not only to translate the artefact and make it accessible in many different languages but also to comment on the video in so-called timed comments, which are displayed at the top of the video or to the right of the video display frame. The twist here is that the comments are tied to the video time rather than the moment in time when the viewer made the comment. When new viewers watch a scene previously commented on, they will be able to read previous viewers' comments about the scene, which creates a pseudo-synchronous effect of co-watching. Locher and Messerli (2020) established that the comments serve a range of functions, from artefact-oriented comments about the plot, genre conventions and actors to more community-oriented comments such as socialising other viewers into understanding how the platform works or revealing where the viewers are from. The most prominent function, though, is sharing emotional reactions such as laughter, fear or disgust (Messerli & Locher 2021). In addition, and counter to the creation of immediacy, historicisation can also take place when past events are brought into the viewing experience. This is the case when commenters write about particular events in their context during their viewing at the time, for example, the beginning of the covid pandemic, the mention of dates of viewing or simply that they are waiting for the next episode to be uploaded. The latter waiting period is not relevant for viewers who watch after the completion of the series. Similar to the interventions of a live audience in a theatre, the effect of the timed comments can thus be to create a joint, co-constructed viewing experience that influences the interpretation of the artefact.

Although we used the 'frozen artefact' metaphor for telecinematic artefacts throughout this Element, we do wish to raise the argument that the audience can turn participatory and change the artefact by adding additional layers of meaning. On platforms such as Viki, viewer roles get blurred with commenter and subtitler roles. In fact, the translations of the artefacts, created by the fan community in Viki, provide a first layer of transformation. The interlingual translations represent an interpretation of the text as well as adding dialogue in the written medium to the retained oral dialogue; furthermore, subtitles are constrained by space restrictions and the need to display them sufficiently long for viewers to read (e.g., Díaz-Cintas & Remael 2007; Guillot 2017, 2020). These subtitles, together with the audio and visual cues from the telecinematic artefact, then form the combined multimodal new artefact. In addition, the content of the timed comments adds yet further information to the artefact, which is then consumed as a whole new artefact by any next viewers. These layers of content have been visualised in Figure 3.

The possibilities of influencing the artefact are also manifest when producers take input from the public into account. For example, movie prescreenings are regularly done to gauge the reaction of the target audience, and in many cases adjustments are made to change the final output (Weaving et al. 2018). The professional and lay discussions in all their manifested forms, from professional article publications to online fan discussions in cyber threads, might be perused by producers when developing the continuation of an ongoing series or contemplating the future of the project in sequels and further seasons (e.g., Oh 2015). In the case of movie adaptations of books or plays, the viewer acclamation might be a driving factor for adopting a project in the first place.

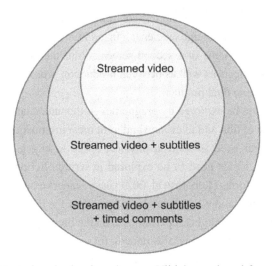

Figure 3 Nested, polyphonic voices on Viki (reproduced from Locher & Messerli 2020: 25)

An important area of research that merges the interest in fiction with how fiction is perceived and consumed has to do with the study of the commercialisation of fiction as a product and fandom in general (Bednarek 2017a, 2017b). Studies on second screen or Locher and Messerli's work on Viki (Locher & Messerli 2020; Messerli & Locher 2021) contribute to this field. Work on fan fiction and spin-offs, intertextuality and establishing influences on interpretation are fruitful further research avenues. Finally, the fairly recent interactive telecinematic artefacts that allow viewers to make choices for the continuation of the story are worth perusing for their meaning-making effects and affordances (Radulovic 2022 on Netflix's products).

4.5 Summary

In this section, we have addressed interaction as an important aspect of engagement with fictional texts. Our understanding of the term has gone beyond interactive books and films – picture books for kids with buttons to press, 'Choose your own adventure' books or telecinematic fiction that changes based on viewer decisions – to understand interaction in a broad sense between authors and artefacts, performers and audiences, viewers and artefacts. As Genette (1982) indicates with his use of the term *palimpsest*, written texts are shaped and transformed by their authors and by other texts. The co-presence characteristic of performed fiction allows some audience interaction in scripted performances, and much more when we turn to improvisation. Telecinematic fiction, finally, spans the whole gamut from private self-controlled viewing settings to cinematic experiences shared by a large audience. In addition, new forms of viewer engagement – on the same or a second screen – blur the boundaries between producers and recipients as well as between production processes of fiction and the no longer quite so final product.

Much remains to be explored by pragmatics in the understanding of collaborative reception of film and television and joint meaning-making in communities that no longer need to share a physical space to engage with fictional artefacts. Similar trends need to be explored in written fiction, where digital social reading platforms (Rebora et al. 2021) have readers exchange their views on books they enjoy, and where e-book readers allow the inclusion of community annotations and highlights superimposed on the literary text. These technological developments, the new affordances for recipients, and the resulting practices change our scholarly understanding of what literary texts are and what fiction is. After all, the applause of the theatre audience, the simplification of a Dickens novel for an easy reader, and the subtitles fans write for Korean TV drama are not themselves fictional. But they create layers of meaning, add voices to artefacts, and redesign them for ever new audiences.

5 Discourse and Ideologies through Character Creation

5.1 Introducing the Connection between Character Creation and Ideologies

In Sections 2, 3 and 4, we focused on participation structure, performance and interaction as issues that are key when fiction and pragmatics are brought together. In this section, we want to explore the idea of story world creation, especially how characters are created in multimodal and linguistic ways and how these characters tap into world-knowledge and ideologies. In doing so, we will also draw on insights from the previous sections.

In a number of instances throughout this Element, this topic has been foreshadowed. For example, in connection with the participation structure, we mentioned that the fictional contract makes it possible for non-fictional world-knowledge to be activated without having to re-enact or re-create the entire contextual knowledge. The fact that a fictional scene plays in France might be established by the use of French music or a picture of the Eiffel tower in the background in a movie, while the location might be simply mentioned in a novel.[5] The frame of a sales interaction

---

[5] This type of constructing, in this case 'Frenchness', is highly conventional in that the creators are arguably mostly concerned with what they believe their target audience would associate with the inclusion of Frenchness on the one hand, and with what has been used in other artefacts to index Frenchness on the other (i.e., existing tropes). For the discussion of including French accent, see Planchenault's work (e.g., 2017). For the inclusion of multilingualism in fiction, see Locher (2017).

might be activated by only showing the payment transaction without having to render the entire dialogue so that the readers and viewers know that they are witnessing an (abbreviated) sales interaction (see, e.g., the discussion of a car sale scene in Messerli 2020). The same shorthand is also possible for character creation. A character might be assigned attributes through cues such as the mention of roles and professions (*detective*), names (*Sherlock*), character traits (*intelligent*), ideological stance (*vegetarian*) etc., they may be given phonological (*accent*), lexical and grammatical features of a dialect to signal a particular standing in society, or they might be even speaking an altogether different language. Importantly, the rendition of the linguistic features need neither be accurate nor complete in comparison to non-fictional renditions in order to contribute to characterisation. What is activated in the readers is the contrast that the features evoke either in comparison to other characters within the artefact (for example, a regional dialect speaker versus a standard dialect speaker) and/or a similarity or contrast of the character with the world-knowledge of the readers'/viewers' own use of language.

A useful distinction can be made between *explicit* and *implicit* characterisation cues (based on Bednarek 2010; Culpeper 2001; Locher & Jucker 2021: ch. 6). Explicit cues can be separated into explicit self-presentation and other-presentation (e.g., characters introduce themselves by name or reveal their age to each other). Implicit cues about a character can be rendered in many different ways, for example through:

- conversational structure (e.g., turn length, turn-taking, turn allocation, topic shift, topic control, incomplete turns/hesitations, interruptions)
- (non-)adherence to conversational maxims, which creates implicatures
- lexis (Germanic vs. Latinate, lexical richness/diversity, surge features/affective language, terms of address, key words)
- syntactic structure
- accent and dialect
- verse and prose
- paralinguistic features (e.g., tempo, pitch range/variation, loudness, voice quality)
- visual features: kinesic features and appearance (e.g., stature, clothing, facial expression, posture)
- context: a character's company and setting
- (im)politeness strategies [. . .] or features (Culpeper 2001: chs. 4–5)

Next to the multimodal indexicals for character creation, such as action, comportment, dress, appearance, etc., the linguistic contrast evoked will contribute to the positioning of characters vis-à-vis each other and vis-à-vis the context in which viewers/readers engage with the artefact. For example, if one reads

Shakespeare's (1596) *A Midsummer Night's Dream,* modern-day readers might perceive contrasts between the main characters (say the Athenians Lysander and Hermia) and the side-plot characters who put on the humorous play-within-the-play (say Peter Quince and Nick Bottom) and might assign the differences to the characters being less educated or belonging to different classes in society. The ways of expressing themselves differ and this contrast is intentionally created for humorous effect. The ways in which the characters are made to speak thus contributes to their characterisation. At the same time, it is possible that some of the features that were tied to particular local and time-dependent readings at the time of Shakespeare are not accessible to today's readers simply because the nuances of what the lexical cues evoke have changed over time. Instead, these readers reinterpret the cues against their own world-knowledge and this reinterpretation might result in new meaning creation.

In the context of plays, we can also draw on the concept of (explicit and implicit) *authorial cues* (Culpeper 2001: 229). They include, for example, the choice of specific proper names in the drama script (which might provide some information on the gender or the nationality of a character, or they may conjure up real-life historical figures) and stage directions (which are sometimes used by playwrights to provide detailed information on the looks, action and comportment of their characters). The information on characterisation is thus given on a different level in the text and not directly in the dialogue. For novels, too, we need to consider different types of narrative voice (Hoffmann 2017) that can reveal explicit and implicit characterisation cues within the telling mode.

Within linguistics, this topic can be linked to the study of identity construction and relational work. The study of identity construction has moved from essentialist approaches that explored style differences and style shifting with simplified categories such as sex, age or class to approaches that look at identity construction as a dynamic process of creating contrasts and evoking meanings which result in dynamic readings of identity (for overviews, see Bucholtz & Hall 2005; Davies & Harré 1990; Locher 2008; Locher & Jucker 2021: ch. 8). It is important to stress that these readings are tied to ideologies of what particular lexical cues signal to their different audiences. So, while identity construction happens in the moment, these readings are not context-free and are in fact culture- and time-bound. Many parameters play into the construction of identity in fiction and non-fiction alike. In Locher and Jucker (2021: 155), this complexity was summarised in an open-ended list of parameters that influence our understanding of the realisation of a particular speech act in its sociocultural context: personal factors, relationship factors, frame factors and the participation structure.

Personal factors are to be seen in connection with the staged face concerns of speakers and addressees. The relationship factors of distance, power, status, affect, density of network and relationship history all influence the choice and interpretation of linguistic strategies. These factors have to be seen in connection with the frames evoked in situ since interactants and staged characters have different roles and rights and obligations that can, e.g., be seen in the sequences of actions that interactants engage in and the subsequent ideologies that are tapped into. Finally, aspects of the participation structure (private communication, the presence of overhearers and witnesses, and whether the interaction is persistent (e.g., letter/email exchanges)) might result in the choice of different linguistic strategies.

In what follows, we further explore the complexity of character creation and its link to ideologies. In Section 5.2, we tap into the potential for studying character creation and the transporting of ideologies in written fiction, with a focus on features of orality. Section 5.3, on performed fiction, deals with the combination of multimodal characterisation cues on the stage, and Section 5.4 turns to multimodality, seriality and translation.

5.2 Written Fiction

Written fiction relies almost entirely on the use of language to create characters. There is no visual mode to show the audience what individual characters look like (but recall the covers mentioned for *Americanah* in Section 2.2), how they behave and what they sound like. It is only when the text is read out that an additional mode comes into play, as for instance in an audiobook or when parents read a bedside story to their child. In this situation, readers can use their voice to portray certain characters in the story world through changing the pitch, the speech tempo, the accent and other aspects of the spoken word. But in the written text, characters must be created through descriptions (telling mode) and through the choice of words characters use in their dialogues (showing mode).

If the authors want to draw attention to a particular way in which words are uttered by a character, they can use specific words that describe ways of speaking or use eye dialect, a term used to show non-standard language usage in written text through non-standard spelling. Consider extracts 5.1 and 5.2, retrieved from the Corpus of Contemporary American English (COCA) (n.d.).

Extract 5.1 'Jury Duty' (Rubin 2018, COCA, fiction)

An older woman with a cloud of gray hair raised her hand. I'm a gardener and this is peak season for flowers, so every day that I'm not at work the flowers are dying, and also I am losing money. But more importantly, the flowers are dying, she implored, passionately.

Extract 5.2 'The Boy Who Stabbed People' (Broumand, 2013, COCA, fiction)

Rella and Pam were always practicing their British accents and considering ways to establish themselves as the natives they should have been. Liverpudlian was best, but tricky; Cockney was encouraged as a reasonable alternative, as were spontaneous references to the East End and having been born near the Bells. 'Muck in yer at yer Granny's!' they shouted to each other, when they remembered, during soccer.

In Extract 5.1, the words by the older woman who wants to be excused from jury duty are described as 'implor[ing] passionately', which may produce an important implicit characterisation cue of the woman. And in Extract 5.2, the author describes the two characters' attempt at producing a British accent with a descriptive passage in which different dialects are mentioned and includes eye dialect, 'Muck in yer at yer Granny's'. Such forms need not be technically accurate as long as they are sufficient to activate the frame of a dialect and thereby characterise the speaker as someone who speaks, or – as in this case – tries to speak, a particular dialect.

David Nicholls' novel *The Understudy*, first published in 2005, focuses on two young actors who could not be more different: on the one hand, there is Josh Harper, a rising megastar who is described as the twelfth sexiest man in the world, and who plays the leading role in a biographical play about Lord Byron in the London West End; on the other hand, there is his understudy, the hapless Stephen C. McQueen, who would be called upon to play his part if Josh were unable to perform on a particular night. They are introduced to the reader in the opening chapters of the novel. The first chapter starts with what looks like a movie script. In a mortuary, two inspectors deliberate the possible causes of death of the murder victim, who is described in the stage directions as 'semi-naked body of a YOUNG MAN, early thirties, his bloated body lying cold and dead on the mortuary slab, in the early stages of decomposition' (Location 70). At this early stage in the novel, the reader does not know that this is actually the introduction of the focaliser of the entire novel through authorial cues in the form of stage directions. The movie script continues for another page or so, when a break in the script makes it clear that a new frame is being activated. In the context of the novel, we were witnessing actors performing a scene for the camera, and we now turn to a scene in which the movie director angrily orders for the scene to be repeated because the corpse had been visibly moving. At this point, the corpse starts speaking and apologises for the mishap.

Extract 5.3 *The Understudy* (Nicholls 2005: Location 77)

'Sorry! Sorry, sorry, everyone,' said the DEAD YOUNG MAN, sitting up and folding his arms self-consciously across his blue painted chest

In this opening scene, the reader gets a large number of authorial and implicit cues that characterise the main character. He is first introduced as a corpse known only as 'dead young man' (an authorial cue), and it takes a while for the reader to realise that the corpse is played by a not very successful actor, because apparently he was doing rather too much while he was supposed to be doing nothing at all and the other actors were busy acting out a fast paced scene. But even as an actor, he seems to be a person without an identity. The director has to ask him for his name ('what's your name, again?' Location 88) when he is in the process of telling him off. The implicit characterisation cues strongly reveal that the role of the corpse is played by a second-rate or perhaps even third-rate actor.

The second chapter starts with what is framed as a newspaper article. Josh Harper is described explicitly as a media star and a most promising young actor (Extract 5.4).

Extract 5.4 *The Understudy* (Nicholls 2005: Location 140)

Still only 28, Josh Harper is Britain's hottest, and prettiest, young actor. Recently voted the 12th Sexiest Man in the World by readers of a well-known women's magazine, he shot to fame four years ago when he became the youngest actor ever to win a BAFTA for his heart-breaking performance as Clarence, the mentally handicapped young man waging a battle with terminal disease, in acclaimed TV drama Seize the Day.

The article also includes interview passages in which Josh adds further explicit cues about himself. Prompted by the journalist, Josh talks not only about his fame and success but also about his happy marriage and his active and satisfying sex life. At this point, the text is interrupted, and the reader realises that the dead young man from the previous chapter had been reading this text with growing impatience and disgust. He is on his way to the theatre for his role as understudy of the megastar he has just been reading about. But he is a few minutes late, and again has to apologise.

Extract 5.5 *The Understudy* (Nicholls 2005: Location 222)

'Phew!' said Stephen. 'It's like Piccadilly Circus out there!'
'Doesn't get any funnier, Stephen.'
'Sorry, Donna, it's the tube . . . '
'Not an acceptable excuse,' grumbled Donna, dialling her mobile.

Donna, the stage manager, is not impressed by the apology, but it still appears that Stephen will get his long-hoped-for chance to step in for Josh, which, he is convinced, would be his breakthrough as an actor. But at the very last moment, Josh also appears, apologising as well, but in a way that shows him for the very different character that he is.

Extract 5.6 *The Understudy* (Nicholls 2005: Location 274)

'Fuck me, bollocks, shit, hi people, sorrysorrysorry I'm late . . .'
. . . and panting, and tossing his hair, the 12th Sexiest Man in the World
tumbled into the dressing room, entering, as always, as if someone had
just thrown him a stick.
Stephen stopped putting on his leather trousers.
'Josh! You were about to give your Aunty Donna a heart attack!' beamed
Donna, skipping to the door and tousling his tremendous hair.

The apologies by Stephen and Josh could not be more different, and they serve as
strong implicit characterisation cues. In his first apology (Extract 5.3), Stephen
apologises profusely with sincere regret for his momentary lack of success in
playing a corpse and doing nothing at all, but his apology is met with annoyance
and sarcasm by the director. In the second apology (Extract 5.5), he tries a more
playful approach and produces what looks like a not really convincing excuse
about the tube. Josh, on the other hand, does not produce any excuses; instead, he
accompanies his apology with a series of swear words in a flamboyant show of his
own importance (Extract 5.6). But this apology is met with joyful concern and
relief by the stage manager. The different rendering of the apologies and the
reactions to the two apologies are thus staged to show how the theatre production
crew holds the two actors in different esteem. Their status and power are shown to
be at opposite ends, reflecting the ideologies of revering the more successful
person (rather than, for example, acknowledging that both work hard).

Thus, through a combination of authorial, explicit and implicit cues, two
characters are being created who share the same profession (acting) but who
otherwise appear to be living in different worlds, both metaphorically and, as
the subsequent chapters will show, also literally in that Stephen lives in a squalid
bedsit while Josh owns a mansion in one of the posh areas of London.

This demonstration of how written cues of different types are used to create
two different main characters serves to demonstrate how the written medium
creatively combines the indexical force of cues to evoke a picture in the readers'
minds. What is activated beyond the linguistic message and contrast itself (such
as the use of swearwords versus their absence) is the staging of power and status
that taps into societal ideologies. In Sections 5.3 and 5.4, we turn to performed
and telecinematic fiction, in which the realisation of characterisation cues may
take very different forms.

5.3 Performed Fiction

While written fiction has to rely on language for creating characters, performed
fiction employs multimodal resources for characterisation. Most crucially, the first

information about characters that is presented to the audience is often the character's appearance. This includes all kinds of embodied clues, such as the character's physicality, facial expression, gestures, ways of moving, voice, dialect and accent, way of speaking, clothing and props. In addition, other multimodal aspects can contribute to characterisation, such as stage design and even music and sound effects. In Section 5.4, we will discuss in more detail how the general setting can bear on character creation. In this section, we focus on character appearance and, especially, the link between the actor's identity and characterisation.

In scripted performed fiction, actors are carefully selected for the roles they perform. Typically, actors tend to be cast in such a way that there is a great deal of similarity between the character and the actor's own identity, especially with respect to identity categories such as sex/gender, age and ethnicity. This means that the actor's appearance provides information about the fictional character, such as the character's age and gender. However, conventions with respect to how much similarity is expected between actor and character vary across different forms of fiction and genres, as well as across aspects of (character) identity, and they have also changed over time. For instance, in Shakespeare's time, women were not allowed on stage, and thus it was the norm that female roles were performed by male actors. This is no longer the case today. Instead, cross-casting in theatre is now used as an artistic tool (see below). The change of such conventions is subject to broader cultural norms. For instance, in the early twentieth century, it was quite common that non-white characters were performed by white actors, a practice that has since come into disrepute as 'whitewashing'. Changes in the casting conventions relating to ethnicity have been closely connected to political movements in the twentieth century, especially the civil rights movement (Pao 2010). One of the most recent areas that has led to heated debates in casting is sex/gender identity. An example of this is Eddie Redmayne's performance of Lili Elbe in *The Danish Girl* (2015). The film presents a fictionalised account of one of the earliest sex-reassignment surgeries, performed on Elbe, who was born male. Redmayne was celebrated and even nominated for an Oscar for this role, but he has also faced heavy criticism for playing the role of a transsexual character as a cis-male actor (BBC News 2021).

A close agreement between the character and the actor's identity is not expected in all areas and contexts, though. In theatre, and especially for the production of great classic plays, there has been a long tradition of casting actors with identities that are markedly different from the character they perform. Not least, this is one of the ways in which new readings of classic plays are created on stage (see also Section 2). A case in point is Shakespeare's *Hamlet*, certainly one of the most coveted roles for theatre actors. In an article from 2019,

The Guardian lists twelve major productions of *Hamlet* since the eighteenth century in which Hamlet was performed by female actors, including two productions with a black female lead (*The Guardian* 2019). Each of these productions exploits the discrepancy between the actor's gender and the gender of the role differently by emphasising certain aspects of physical appearance and character attributes that are or are not typically associated with female gender. Extracts 5.7, 5.8 and 5.9, from critical reviews of four productions, illustrate this point.

> Extract 5.7 Hamlet review – Maxine Peake is a delicately ferocious Prince of Denmark (Clapp 2014)
>
> [Maxine Peake] wears a dark blue trouser suit that might have been imagined by a fashion-conscious Chairman Mao. She is a stripling prince, almost presexual, who glides, without swagger and without girlishness.
>
> Extract 5.8 Hamlet/Richard III review – Ruth Negga plays the Prince with priceless precision (Billington 2018)
>
> The Irish-Ethiopian Negga's Hamlet is a fascinating mix of male and female: a dark-suited, swift-spoken, ferociously intelligent figure who sees both through Elsinore's corruption and his/her inability to counter it.
>
> Extract 5.9 Hamlet review – this fresh prince is fully and gloriously female (Love 2019)
>
> [...] Hamlet is allowed to be fully female; there is no suggestion that Tessa Parr is playing the part of a man, and nor does her performance suggest the kind of androgyny embraced by Maxine Peake in the same role. Instead, Hamlet is immediately established as a woman, opening the play to a fascinating series of new possibilities. Lines such as 'frailty, thy name is woman' hit the ear differently.

In the production discussed in Extract 5.7, the gender identity of both the performer and the role are backgrounded through an androgynous presentation, whereas the production discussed in Extract 5.8 combines selected aspects that are perceived as male and female. In Extract 5.9, finally, the role is reinterpreted as a female role to the extent that the script is adjusted accordingly. In all these productions, the audience perceives certain aspects of the actor's female identity as an additional layer of meaning that offers new perspectives on a classic text.

In contrast to scripted performance, in improvised theatre the expectation that the actor's identity and appearance provide information about the character is suspended. Since the content of the scenes is not known before the performance, actors have to be prepared to perform any role that might come up, and it is common for actors to perform more than one role within an improvised performance or even within the same scene. Thus, it is part of the fictional contract with the audience that any performer can perform any type of character. Except for genre-based improvisation theatre, such as improvised Shakespeare or improvised Hitchcock, most improvised theatre takes place on a bare stage without props and costumes. This leaves only two resources for creating characters, language and the presentation of physicality through acting. Language can be used for characterisation in two ways. Implicit cues can reveal character information through use of accent and dialect, lexis, syntactic structure, etc., as discussed in Sections 5.1 and 5.2. In addition, language is used for explicit characterisation in what improvisers call 'definition' of characters (Sawyer 2003: 112–15). Such instances of direct verbal characterisation are usually delivered in the form of character dialogue, and a character can be defined by any of the performers on stage (on the functions of dialogue in fiction, see Bednarek 2017c, 2018: 33–77; Kozloff 2000; Locher & Jucker 2021: 128). In contrast to verbal definitions, implicit verbal cues and characterisation through acting are much more open to interpretation. They invite the audience and the co-performers to make assumptions about a character, which can then be confirmed or contradicted by explicit verbal definitions. Throughout the performance, different types of character cues are accumulated, defining the characters in increasing detail and depth.

The ways in which implicit characterisation and verbal definitions interact in improvised theatre can be illustrated with the opening passage from a performance by Katy Schutte and Rachel Blackman. The two actors start their performance without taking any audience suggestions, and thus there are no pre-set expectations with respect to the setting and characters that are being presented. At the beginning of each performance, each actor positions herself on stage, sometimes mirroring the position of the other performer, sometimes adopting a complementary stance. The way in which the two characters are positioned to each other – which is not discussed beforehand between the performers – provides the initial inspiration for the setting and the characters. In a show that was only retrospectively entitled *Playing Field*, the two actors sit on two chairs at a distance from each other when the lights go up (see Figure 4). The first lines that are spoken are presented in Extract 5.10.

Extract 5.10 *Katy & Rach: Playing Field* (2021), 29 September, 00:01:30–00:02:55

1 KS: He's good. (gesturing towards the audience)
2 RB: Yeah.
3 KS: Mine's a bit more awkward.
4 RB: Is this your first time?
5 KS: Yeah, it's the first time he got in the game, so –
6 RB: Oh.

Figure 4 Rachel Blackman (left) and Katy Schutte in the opening scene of *Katy & Rach: Playing Field* (2021) (reproduced with permission)

7 KS: Yeah, I'm a bit nervous.
8 RB: Yeah yeah yeah. I've been coming for about five years now. I mean,
9   we've been coming, you know. (gesturing towards the audience)
10 KS: Oh wow.
11 [...]
12 RB: So I mean obviously, um, I don't want to boast. I know every parent
13   thinks their kid's the most impressive. But um, but um, my child,
14   Colin, he's the one with the red hair?
15 KS: Oh yeah.
16 RB: He's very quick. He's very good.
17 [...]
18 RB: He's very very quick and I mean we think he's gonna be playing
19   professionally within a few years.

This passage provides some explicit information about the two characters and their setting. We learn that Rachel's character (RB) has a child named Colin (line 14) and that RB thinks that Colin is 'very good' (line 16). We also learn that RB and Colin have been coming to this place for about five years already, whereas Katy's character (KS) is here for the first time. There is no explicit verbal definition of the location, but the way in which the two performers gaze into the audience space and the expression 'playing professionally' suggest a sports site.

The interaction following this passage confirms the assumption that we are at a sports site by providing verbal definitions ('kick', 'ball', 'Premier League') that establish the activity as a children's football game. With respect to the character RB, there is not much additional explicit characterisation for quite some time. Most characterisation takes place through implicit cues. RB's posture is broad-legged (see Figure 4) and RB shows some male-connotated behaviour, such as scratching, drinking out of a can and aggressive shouting at the game in the continuation of the scene. Implicit linguistic clues reinforce this impression. Whereas KS uses *sweetie*, *honey* and *darling* to call out to her child – terms of endearment that are associated with mothers more than with fathers – RB calls Colin by his first name. However, it is not until 00:08:15, when the two characters introduce themselves to each other as Lilly (KS) and Adam (RB), that RB is defined as male. At that point, it would still be perfectly possible for the performers to assign a female name to RB, which would require the audience to adjust their conception of the character that they had formed based on implicit cues.

In sum, performed fiction establishes characters through a combination of implicit and explicit visual and verbal cues. The use of these cues as well as the role of the actor's identity vary across different forms of performed fiction, as well as across different genres and styles. Improvised theatre presents particularly intriguing material for the study of fictional characterisation, given that we can observe how characters are built up incrementally through different types of explicit and implicit, verbal and non-verbal cues over the course of a performance.

5.4 Telecinematic Fiction

In Section 3.4, we already mentioned the multimodal nature of telecinematic artefacts as their key distinguishing factor in comparison to written fiction. This general comment also bears on character creation within the telecinematic artefact. Even more so than in performed fiction such as rehearsed and impro-vised theatre, the collective producers of the telecinematic artefact can draw on a plethora of cues that tap into ideologies which jointly create meaning in creative ways. In what follows, we raise this aspect of multimodality, but also seriality, translation and interaction as issues we consider worth exploring further in this field.

We first turn to staged character change within an artefact that draws on multimodality. Locher and Jucker (2021: 106–8) used the example of the play *Pygmalion* by Bernard Shaw ([1914] 1983) to discuss how the transformation of the London working-class girl Eliza Doolittle into a woman who can pull off appearing like a lady of the English upper classes involves training her to speak differently and thus to style-shift. Linguistic cues are thus exploited to index class difference, and in this case, this is an explicit part of the plot of the play. In addition, Eliza's ways of dressing and comporting herself are changed and her world-knowledge is widened. In this type of play, appearance, action and language together are staged to show change within the same character within the enactment of the duration of the written play (authorial cues are given in the stage directions) and its performed versions as theatre production, musical adaptation and movie version. While not every fictional artefact has the transformation of its (main) characters as a theme, the multimodal nature of both performed fiction and telecinematic fiction allow this change to be expressed in more than linguistic ways, such as the clothes the characters get to wear, their living conditions and possession of status symbols.

To give another example, the main female character Maureen Murphy Quinn in the US movie *She's So Lovely* (1997) is first shown to be living together with her first husband in a squalid New York apartment, smoking and drinking. After an escalation of violence, Maureen's husband is imprisoned. The movie then moves forward in time and we see Maureen in an entirely different light to the extent that she is barely recognisable at first: she has a different hairstyle and hair colour, wears different clothes and serves breakfast to her three children. It becomes clear that she has remarried and lives in an affluent suburb in a house with a swimming pool and has transformed herself entirely (only to go back to her first husband in the continuation of the movie when it becomes clear that the transformation was in fact superficial and temporary). The suburban setting signifies a safe living situation that is full of status symbols. This setting, however, gains its particular significance for the plot due to the contrast with the beginning of the movie. What this example shows is the complex interplay of characterisation cues on many levels that index character change and character contrast (Mittell 2015: 134–5).

In the two examples just given, the transformation of characters is staged within one play (and its adaptations) and movie. Change in characterisation, however, can also be built up over time in the format of a series. Publishing in instalments has a long-standing tradition in writing, such as Charles Dickens' novels, the chapters of which were published in magazines and ended in cliffhangers that enticed their readers to keep reading. Comic books and manga series, children's book series and detective novel series come easily to mind. Seriality within the telecinematic format has an equally long tradition and has been explored in recent times in different ways. For example, creators have added seasons of television series to streaming sites episode by episode or in bulk, they have released sequels to films and also movies set before these films (prequels), and they have created movies and series based on minor or new characters that share the same story world (spin-offs and cinematic universes, as, for example, Marvel's). With respect to characterisation, this episodic development of plot lines means that the characters can be built up more slowly and incrementally. Depending on the genre, however, character change is more or less prominent. In traditional multicamera sitcoms, for instance, characters often remain fairly static. While Mittell (2015: 133) finds that to be true for serial narratives more generally, other serialised genres than sitcoms, such as coming-of-age series, are more prone to display character change, as it is the main focus of the narrative. In general, distinctions can also be made between main characters who have more detailed and round profiles and characters of secondary or marginal importance who remain more flat.

In her study on the US series *Gilmore Girls* (2000–2007), Bednarek (2010, 2011) explores characterisation from many different angles, including linguistic and multimodal behaviour. She draws on corpus linguistics and pragmatics to explore differences in language use and expression of emotional stance by the main characters. Bednarek (2010: 106) also wonders whether the reported impression that 'there is clearly a need for consistency of voice in terms of characterization and identification' is indeed true or whether the main characters' linguistic profiles changed during the course of the *Gilmore Girls* series (Bednarck 2011). Her analyses did not show significant stylistic change, but some character change on the level of lexis can be explained with different topics discussed over the seasons or with introducing characters at the beginning of the series. The fairly static linguistic description of character depiction might therefore be indeed typical of telecinematic discourse, an aspect worth exploring further.

The various forms of seriality are a particularly interesting arena for characterisation. Prequels like the second *Star Wars*[6] trilogy juxtapose two competing chronologies: the past of the story world meets the future of the viewing experience. Viewers already have existing models of the famous characters that populate that galaxy far, far away – they know the Skywalker siblings and Han Solo, and the epic adventures they had together. The characters in the prequels themselves, however, are oblivious to their inevitable future filmed two decades earlier. As a result, viewers join the collective sender in a privileged position, from which they flesh out that particular galactic prehistory, enjoying how the puzzle pieces fall into place and result in a more complex character creation with more detail.

A different type of spin-off is not set before or after events already shared, but is set at the same time as a previously published artefact. This allows (aspects of)

---

[6] The first published trilogy of the *Star Wars* series consists of *Star Wars Episode IV: A New Hope* (1977), *Star Wars Episode V: The Empire Strikes Back* (1980) and *Star Wars Episode VI: Return of the Jedi* (1983). Then, movies appeared in the form of a prequel trilogy, i.e., the events of the films occur before the intradiegetic time of the first trilogy: *Star Wars Episode I: The Phantom Menace* (1999), *Star Wars Episode II: Attack of the Clones* (2002), and *Star Wars Episode III: Revenge of the Sith* (2005). The entire set, in turn, was followed by another sequel trilogy: *Star Wars Episode VII: The Force Awakens* (2015), *Star Wars Episode VIII: The Last Jedi* (2017), and *Star Wars Episode IX: The Rise of Skywalker* (2019).

the same story to be told through different focalisers. Encountering already-known characters from a different perspective adds depth to the characters. Examples that come to mind from written and performed fiction are E. L. James' *Fifty Shades of Grey* novel series (James 2012, 2021), in which the first trilogy and second trilogy are written from the perspective of different characters on the same events, or Gregory Maguire's (1995) novel *Wicked* and its later Broadway musical adaptation (Schwartz & Holzman 2003), in which the well-known *The Wonderful Wizard of Oz* (Baum [1900] 2000) is retold from the perspective of the minor character Elphaba, the Wicked Witch of the West. The *Star Wars* universe also includes such a spin-off: rather than being set before or after events already shared, *Rogue One: A Star Wars Story* returns to the time of the very first film, *A New Hope*, to explain the building and destruction of the Death Star, that ominous space station and weapon that creates much of the suspense in the original *Star Wars* films.

In the *Star Wars* sequels, viewers ask themselves how Darth Vader became the nemesis of his own son, how one tiny ship could destroy an entire space station, how events might have affected different characters in the story world. Scholarship in pragmatics needs to ask: how do we (re-)conceptualise characters when they appear in new stories and are played by different actors? How do storytellers navigate characters between diegetic cause and effect (for example, the events that made Anakin Skywalker turn evil) and film series dramaturgy (for example, how viewers expect characters to behave based on how their future selves acted in previous films)? Similar questions can also be asked for other serial formats, made by both professionals and fans, which add new elements to story worlds and adopt and adapt the characters that animate them.

A further point worth exploring is the challenge of translating linguistic characterisation cues. As pointed out before, features of dialogue can be used to position characters with respect to their standing vis-à-vis others. Syntactic, phonological and lexical features might be employed to index regional, social and ethnic belonging, etc. However, these indexes are tied to these regions and their populations in a particular time. As a consequence, it is not self-evident how to translate regional cues (say Hagrid in the *Harry Potter* book and movie series (Rowling 1997)) or ethnic cues (say Toni Morrison's (1987) characters in *Beloved* in book and movie form). Queen (2004), in her study on how African American Vernacular speakers in US movies were given a German voice in dubbing, explains that no regional German dialect and no German ethnic dialect was available that would index comparable notions. To solve this, the translators followed a line of approximation: 'if the character being dubbed is young, male and tied to the street cultures of the urban inner city, then AAE is dubbed using a form of German that has links to the urban youth cultures of north-central Germany' (Queen 2004: 515). As a consequence, some of the characters' make-up is retained while other aspects are dropped.

How to creatively deal with characterisation in translation, dubbing and subtitling is also explored in Locher (2020), where linguistic relationship negotiations by characters through the discussion of address terms and politeness levels in Korean is translated into English subtitles. The practices show that, for example, some of the Korean address terms that do not exist in English are retained as Korean borrowings in the subtitles and that the subtitlers also make use of comments in brackets to flag or explain relational meaning as expressed in different politeness levels indexed in grammatical morphemes in Korean that cannot be translated into English morphemes. In Swiss films, Messerli (2019) has shown that English subtitles present a form of authorial summary (i.e., an interpretation) that accompanies the multitude of voices present in film and preprocesses meaning, including the understanding of characters. The nuances and possibilities of exploiting often subtle linguistic cues for characterisation thus pose a challenge for translators and ask for creative solutions.

Finally, to make a link to Section 4 on interaction, Locher and Messerli (2020) and Messerli and Locher (2021) give evidence that viewers of the aforementioned Korean dramas often pick up on characterisation nuances and comment on them by asking questions about the character positionings (such as 'were they not formal before'). In non-fictional and fictional life alike, these positioning cues are important and consumers of fictional artefacts show awareness of this fact.

5.5 Summary

In this section, we explored the many cues for characterisation offered to readers and viewers to form a mental picture of the character, which can be incrementally built up. Crucially, these cues evoke characteristics that can be linked to particular ideologies. The cues are thus strategically placed to create contrasts between characters in the intradiegetic world and contrasts to potentially targeted readers or viewers.

It is also worth exploring further how story world creation is being mutually created by story location, time and character positionings. For example, in improvised theatre forms that start without a suggested location, the performance of the characters creates the story world location and setting, rather than the story world being suggested by a narrator in a novel or the visual input of stage props or a movie location that is then populated by characters. How these paths for story world creation influence the creation of meaning and understanding is worth exploring further.

For performed and telecinematic fiction, we particularly highlighted the interplay of multimodal cues and explored the complex interplay between them. So far, most linguistic studies of characterisation have focused on written fiction and on explicit and implicit linguistic cues in telecinematic fiction. We argue that the interplay between visual and verbal characterisation is a promising field for multimodal pragmatics.

Finally, we made links to participation structure (Section 2) and interaction (Section 4) by highlighting how translation and reader/viewer interaction can impact characterisation. This is a field that we could only touch on here, but that has potential for more explorations with a pragmatic lens.

6 Conclusions and Outlook

6.1 Pragmatics and Fiction

Our aims in this Element were to convince its readers that the study of fictional data can be explored with key concepts from pragmatics in order to understand fiction as practice but also to further pragmatic theorising. By necessity, we had to make a strategic choice about what to highlight out of the many options for exploration. Our choice fell on participation structure, performance and interaction, as well as characterisation and ideologies.

Our discussions have shown that the first three concepts are intricately intertwined and connected. The discussion of the participation structure by necessity explores the context for performance and interaction. Performance cannot be explained without establishing who is part of the participation structure and who can interact with each other. Finally, giving interaction centre stage cannot be done without thinking of the previous two concepts. Despite the fact that it might thus seem counter-intuitive to separate these concepts at first sight, we have chosen to explore each of the concepts in the context of three very broad types of fiction: written, performed and telecinematic. This approach has allowed us to juxtapose how these forms of fiction differ when explored through a particular lens.

Our findings reveal that it is worthwhile to define the different participation structures by drawing on concepts such as paratext, intertextuality, and audience design and the fictional contract, which guides readers' and viewers' interpretations of the text as fiction. The concept of performance cannot only be meaningfully explored for live theatre productions but is also worth studying in written and telecinematic texts, where textual and multimodal cues are combined in different ways to create performed effects for recipients. While interaction immediately comes to mind when thinking of live theatre perform-ances, where audience members can co-shape the happenings on the stage, it also proved fruitful for written fiction when combined with the idea of inter-textuality and paratext, both diachronically and synchronically. We were also able to show that telecinematic artefacts can be meaningfully discussed with the concept of interaction by exploring how audiences react to texts (e.g., as critics or with online comments), co-write texts (e.g., in spin-offs and fan fiction) and influence ongoing serials with feedback. In addition, we showed how watching on one's own or in a group (online or in the same physical location) changes how the artefact is experienced.

The last point brings us back to the interconnectedness of the concepts of participation structure, performance and interaction, and allows us to emphasise the fuzzy borders between the different fictional types that we had set up with a big brush. While it is useful to think in the categories of written, performed and telecinematic in light of their mediality, our discussion demonstrates to what extent each of these types is embedded in cultural meaning-making processes that are shaped by participation structure, performance and interaction. Readers and viewers experience and interpret fiction against a complex backdrop of individual, situated life experience that is shaped by a particular society's norms and ideologies.

It is therefore not coincidental, and far from being an afterthought, that we singled out characterisation and its link to ideologies as one key element of fiction in Section 5. On the one hand, the choice to explore characterisa-tion was motivated by the importance that characters and their creation have in fiction as one crucial aspect of story world creation and plot advancement. On the other hand, the discussion of characterisation allowed us to show how the concepts of participation structure, performance and interaction are intertwined and can result in effects for characterisation. When characters are contrasted within the intradiegetic world in their ways of speaking and interacting, this is pitched against the viewers' and readers' (changing) contexts and ideologies. Our discussion of interaction in Section 5 shows to what extent recipients can become part of shaping characters so that the artefacts themselves lose some of their defined borders and become fuzzy.

6.2 Outlook

Much more remains to be done in this line of research. In many of our sections, we discussed more issues and nuances among ourselves than there was space to include in this Element. In what follows, we wish to highlight a number of these research avenues. These are meant to be pointers and the list is by no means closed.

The concept of narrative is one of the core concepts that we could not introduce in detail in this Element due to space reasons. This concept, however, is a fundamental discourse unit that people draw on in fictional and non-fictional contexts (see Locher & Jucker 2021: ch. 5). The topic of narratives also has a long tradition in sociolinguistic, pragmatic and discourse studies that explore especially personal high point narratives, but also how small stories and tiny stories emerge in everyday life (e.g., Dayter 2016; Georgakopoulou 2007; Labov 1972). How readers and viewers draw on their knowledge of non-fictional storytelling when interpreting fictional narratives, how they draw on the fictional contract when interpreting cues not only of characterisation but story world creation (e.g., Gavins 2007) in general, and how these processes differ in written, performed and telecinematic artefacts remains a fascinating research area. Further key concepts for studying fiction from a pragmatic angle are genre (how are genre conventions re-created, changed and exploited?) and emotions (how are emotions shown and told in different types of data?) (see Section 1.1; Locher & Jucker 2021: chs. 4, 9).

With respect to characterisation, there are a number of interesting scenarios to explore that can be discussed with the fictional contract in mind. In Section 5, we mentioned that casting traditions for the stage and film can change over time. For example, the viewers accepted that men played women on the Shakespearean stage or that an established theatre ensemble distributes roles among themselves even when the physical appearance does not match. An actor in their thirties might be asked to play a high school student or a grandmother, depending on the demands of the role. While social variables such as age, gender and ethnicity might be treated more liberally in some instances, language is given a particular importance within characterisation for the stage and film in some cases. This can be seen in the considerable effort that is invested in some projects for actors to be able to explore the power of linguistic indexicalities by engaging voice coaches to teach accents and dialect/sociolect variation, different languages being included or entirely new languages being invented (see Bleichenbacher 2008; Locher 2017). However, there are also counter-examples where linguistic variability is levelled and multilingual situations are glossed over. There thus seem to be different ideologies at work in connection with how much distance between character and actor is traditionally acceptable, and what particular code of realism fictional artefacts orient to. As stated before, an actual match of the fictional language with the language used in non-fictional contexts is not necessary to draw on the effects of indexicality for story world creation. How changing ideologies affect the fictional contract with respect to characterisation remains a rich research area for pragmatics.

In addition, we see great potential for pragmatic research in exploring emerging ideologies not only within a fictional artefact (see Locher & Jucker 2021: ch. 8) but also around fiction by exploring the meta-discourses that recipients engage in. How do lay and scholarly recipients of fiction engage with fiction, write about fiction and exchange ideas about fiction? How are fandoms created and maintained? How do the possibilities and affordances of engaging in this meta-discourse across time and space change? Next to the pointers already given in Section 4 about the study of fandoms, further useful concepts that have been applied in other contexts in pragmatics are discourse community (Watts 2008), community of practice (Eckert & McConnell-Ginet 1992), imagined community (Cochrane 2017) and affinity space (Gee 2005).

Thinking about methodology and research design, our discussions around participation structure, performance and interaction have also shown that we always need to be clear about what we actually consider as 'data' for our research project. For written fiction, we need to be clear whether we work on a facsimile of the authors' original texts or maybe notes and drafts that lead to this text, whether we work with editions, adaptations or translations and whether we take the paratext into account. Moreover, we may choose to limit ourselves to text and paratext, or instead be interested also in reader reception. For performed theatre, we need to make decisions as to whether we work with the written published drama text only (taking the same points into account as just mentioned for written fiction) or whether we work with audiovisual recordings of rehearsals or performances in front of an audience, including maybe fieldnotes and interviews, in order to capture the negotiations around language in its multimodal context. Telecinematic artefacts, too, consist of different multilayered types of data, ranging from the written script to the frozen artefact, and fieldnotes and recordings of all the steps in between that contribute to and lead to the frozen artefact. If we are interested in meta-discourses around fiction, our potential data sources increase even further, including reviews by critics and lay people, internet fora for fan clubs, scholarly discussion about fiction, etc. Depending on what scholars wish to research, a combination of different data sets is called for and different methodologies can be combined to explore them.

This list of further inroads for pragmatics into studying fiction is by no means conclusive. We hope that we have been able to show throughout this

Element that we can learn more about fiction by drawing on pragmatics, but that we can also contribute to current discussions in pragmatics by looking at fiction as data and by considering the creation of and engaging with fiction as a fundamental human endeavour that is worth being explored in its own right.

References

Fictional Sources

Adams, Douglas. ([1979] 2005). *The Hitchhiker's Guide to the Galaxy*. New York: Del Rey Ballantine Books.

Adichie, Chimamanda Ngozi. (2013). *Americanah*. New York: Anchor Books.

Austen, Jane. (1813). *Pride and Prejudice*. London: T. Egerton.

Avatar. (2009). Dir. James Cameron. Twentieth Century Fox.

Baum, Frank L. ([1900] 2000). *The Wonderful Wizard of Oz*. New York: Norton

Blade Runner. (1982). Dir. Ridley Scott. Warner Bros.

Brazil. (1985). Dir. Terry Gilliam. Universal Pictures.

Broumand, Lorie. (2013). The boy who stabbed people. *Confrontation* 114, 37–47.

Chaucer, Geoffrey. (1987). *The Canterbury Tales*. In Larry D. Benson (Ed.), *The Riverside Chaucer*. Third edition. Boston, MA: Houghton Mifflin.

Death Becomes Her. (1992). Dir. Robert Zemeckis. Universal Pictures.

Devil's Daughter. (2021). Improvised performance by Devil's Daughter. Annoyance Theatre, Chicago, IL, 3 November.

Ella & Stacey – Close Quarters: Church. (2021a). Improvised performance by Ella Galt and Stacey Smith. Theater Ida, Zurich, 14 August.

Ella & Stacey – Close Quarters: Cruise Ship. (2021b). Improvised performance by Ella Galt and Stacey Smith. Theater Ida, Zurich, 15 August.

Family Dinner. (2021). Improvised performance produced by Molly Ritchie and performed by Family Dinner ensemble. HUGE Improv Theatre, Minneapolis, MN, 5 November.

Fuck This Week. (2021). Improvised performance by Fuck This Week. Fallout Theatre, Austin, TX, 15 November.

Gilmore Girls. (2000–2007). Prod. Gavin Polone, Amy Sherman-Palladino, Patricia Fass Palmer, et al. Warner Bros.

Groundhog Day. (1993). Dir. Harold Ramis. Movies Anywhere.

Hitch*Cocktails. (2021). Improvised performance by Hitch*Cocktails. Annoyance Theatre, Chicago, IL, 21 October.

James, E. L. (2012) *The Fifty Shades of Grey Trilogy*. New York: Penguin Random House.

James, E. L. (2021). *The Fifty Shades of Grey as Told by Christian Trilogy: Grey, Darker, Freed*. New York: Penguin Random House.

Kästner, Erich. (2015). *Lisa and Lottie*. New York: Lizzie Skurnick Books. (Original work published in German in 1949 as *Das Doppelte Lottchen*.)

Katy & Rach: Playing Field. (2021). Improvised performance by Katy Schutte and Rachel Blackwell. Theater Ida, Zurich, 29 September.

Maguire, Gregory. (1995). *Wicked: The Life and Times of the Wicked Witch of the West*. New York: Regan Books.

Middleditch & Schwartz: Parking Lot Wedding. (2020). Improvised performance by Thomas Middleditch and Ben Schwartz. Netflix. www.netflix.com/watch/81140289?trackId=255824129 (last accessed 2 December 2022).

MOLLY. (2021). Improvised performance by Susan Messing and Norm Holly. Annoyance Theatre, Chicago, IL, 24 October.

Morrison, Toni (1987). *Beloved*. New York: Knopf.

Nicholls, David. (2005). *The Understudy*. London: Hodder & Stoughton.

Poe, Edgar Allen. (1967). *Selected Writings of Edgar Allan Poe, Poems, Tales, Essays and Reviews*. David Galloway (ed.). Harmondsworth, UK: Penguin Books.

Prebble, Lucy. (2016). *The Effect*. London: Bloomsbury.

Psycho. (1960). Dir. Alfred Hitchcock. Paramount Pictures.

Psycho. (1998). Dir. Gus Van Sant. Universal Pictures.

Rooney, Sally. (2021). *Beautiful World, Where Are You*. London: Faber & Faber.

Rowling, J. K. (1997). *Harry Potter and the Philosopher's Stone*. London: Bloomsbury.

Rubin, Marina. (2018). Jury Duty. *Pennsylvania Literary Journal*, 10(3), 143–59.

Schwartz, Stephen & Holzman, Winnie. (2003). *Wicked*. Broadway musical.

Scott Pilgrim vs. the World. (2010). Dir. Edgar Wright. Universal Pictures.

Shakespeare, William. ([1596] 2009). *A Midsummer Night's Dream*. John Dover Wilson (Ed.). Cambridge: Cambridge University Press.

Shaw, George Bernard. ([1914] 1983). *Pygmalion*. London: Penguin.

Sherlock (2010–2017). Prod. Steven Moffat, Mark Gatiss, Beryl Vertue, et al. Hartswood Films.

She's So Lovely. (1997). Dir. Nick Cassavetes. Prod. John Cassavetes. Miramax.

Sneakers. (1992). Dir. Phil Alden Robinson. Universal Pictures.

Sophocles. (2000). *The Three Theban Plays: Antigone; Oedipus the King; Oedipus at Colonus*. Robert Fagles (Trans.), Bernard Knox (Introduction). New York: Penguin Classics.

Star Wars (1977). *A New Hope* (later entitled IV) [Film]. Dir. George Lucas. Lucasfilm.

Star Wars (1980). *The Empire Strikes Back* (later entitled V) [Film]. Dir. Irvin Kershner. Lucasfilm.

Star Wars (1983). *Return of the Jedi* (later entitled VI) [Film]. Dir. Richard Marquand. Lucasfilm.

Star Wars (1999). *Episode I: The Phantom Menace* [Film]. Dir. George Lucas. Lucasfilm.

Star Wars (2002). *Episode II: Attack of the Clones* [Film]. Dir. George Lucas. Lucasfilm.

Star Wars (2005). *Episode III: Revenge of the Sith* [Film]. Dir. George Lucas. Lucasfilm.

Star Wars (2015). *Episode VII: The Force Awakens* [Film]. Dir. J. J. Abrams. Lucasfilm.

Star Wars (2016). *Rogue One: A Star Wars Story.* Dir. Gareth Edwards. Lucasfilm.

Star Wars (2017). *Episode VIII: The Last Jedi* [Film]. Dir. Rian Johnson. Lucasfilm.

Star Wars (2019). *Episode IX: The Rise of Skywalker* [Film]. Dir. J. J. Abrams. Lucasfilm.

Super Human. (2021). Improvised performance by Super Human. Annoyance Theatre, Chicago, IL, 27 October.

Super Scene. (2021). Improvised performance by BATS Improv, San Francisco, CA, 4 December.

The Cabinet of Dr. Caligari. (1920). Dir. Robert Wiene. Decla-Bioscop.

The Danish Girl. (2015). Dir. Tom Hooper. Universal Pictures.

The Parent Trap. (1998). Dir. Nancy Meyers. Buena Vista Pictures.

The Wire. (2002–2008). Prod. Karen L. Thorson, Nina K. Noble, David Simon, et al. HBO.

The Witcher. (2019). Prod. Steve Gaub, Jason F. Brown, Tomasz Baginski, et al. Netflix.

TJ & Dave: Blurting in Earnest. (2016). Improvised performance by TJ Jagodowski and Dave Pasquesi. Clark Street Films: Vimeo. https://vimeo.com/ondemand/tjanddave/118665656 (last accessed 2 December 2022).

Secondary Sources

Alvarez-Pereyre, Michael. (2011). Using film as linguistic specimen: Theoretical and practical issues. In Roberta Piazza, Monika Bednarek, & Fabio Rossi (Eds.), *Telecinematic Discourse. Approaches to the Language of Films and Television Series* (pp. 47–67). Amsterdam: John Benjamin.

Androutsopoulos, Jannis, & Weidenhöffer, Jessica. (2015). Zuschauer-Engagement auf Twitter: Handlungskategorien der rezeptionsbegleitenden Kommunikation am Beispiel von #tatort. *Zeitschrift für angewandte Linguistik*, 62(1), 23–59.

Barthes, Roland. (1970). *S/Z*. Paris: Éditions du seuil.

Bauman, Richard. (2000). Language, identity, performance. *Pragmatics* 10(1), 1–5.

Bazin, André. ([1958] 1960). The ontology of the photographic image. H. Gray (Trans.). *Film Quarterly*, 13(4), 4–9.

BBC News. (2021). Eddie Redmayne says it was a mistake to play trans role in The Danish Girl. *BBC News*, 22 November, www.bbc.com/news/entertainment-arts-59373295 (last accessed 18 February 2022).

Bednarek, Monika A. (2010). *The Language of Fictional Television: Drama and Identity*. London: Continuum.

Bednarek, Monika A. (2011). The stability of the televisual character: A corpus stylistic case study. In Roberta Piazza, Monika Bednarek, & Fabio Rossi (Eds.), *Telecinematic Discourse: Approaches to the Language of Films and Television Series* (pp. 185–204). Amsterdam: John Benjamin.

Bednarek, Monika A. (2017a). (Re)circulating popular television: Audience engagement and corporate practices. In Janus Mortensen, Nikolas Coupland, & Jacob Thogersen (Eds.), *Style, Mediation, and Change: Sociolinguistic Perspectives on Talking Media* (pp. 115–40). New York: Oxford University Press.

Bednarek, Monika A. (2017b). Fandom. In Christian Hoffmann & Wolfram Bublitz (Eds.), *Pragmatics of Social Media* (pp. 545–72). Berlin: De Gruyter Mouton.

Bednarek, Monika A. (2017c). The role of dialogue in fiction. In Miriam A. Locher & Andreas H. Jucker (Eds.), *Pragmatics of Fiction* (Handbooks of Pragmatics 12) (pp. 129–58). Berlin: De Gruyter Mouton.

Bednarek, Monika A. (2018). *Language and Television Series: A Linguistic Approach to TV Dialogue*. Cambridge: Cambridge University Press.

Bednarek, Monika A. (2019). *Creating Dialogue For TV: Screenwriters Talk Television*. Abingdon: Routledge.

Bell, Allan. (1991). *The Language of News Media*. Oxford: Basil Blackwell.

Billington, Michael. (2018). Hamlet/Richard III review: Ruth Negga plays the Prince with priceless precision. *The Guardian*, 7 October 2019, https://bit.ly/3F6Dgct (last accessed 18 February 2022).

Bleichenbacher, Lukas. (2008). *Multilingualism in the Movies. Hollywood Characters and their Language Choices* (Vol. 135). Tübingen: Narr Francke.

Bordwell, David, Thompson, Kristin, & Smith, Jeff (2020). *Film Art: An Introduction*. Twelfth edition. New York: McGraw-Hill Education.

Brock, Alexander. (2015). Participation framworks and participation in televised sitcom, candid camera and stand-up comedy. In Marta Dynel and Jan Chovanec

(Eds.), *Participation in Public and Social Media Interactions*. (Pragmatics & Beyond New Series 256) (pp. 27–47). Amsterdam: John Benjamins.

Broth, Mathias. (2011). The theatre performance as interaction between actors and their audience. *Nottingham French Studies* 50(2), 113–33.

Brubaker, David (1993). André Bazin on automatically made images. *The Journal of Aesthetics and Art Criticism* 51(1), 59–67.

Bubel, Claudia M. (2006). The linguistic construction of character relations in TV drama: Doing friendship in *Sex and the City*. (PhD), Universität des Saarlandes. https://bit.ly/3ALpARy (last accessed 30 November 2022).

Bubel, Claudia M. (2008) Film audiences as overhearers. *Journal of Pragmatics* 40(1), 55–71.

Bublitz, Wolfram. (2017). Oral features in fiction. In Miriam A. Locher & Andreas H. Jucker (Eds.), *Pragmatics of Fiction* (pp. 235–63). Berlin: De Gruyter Mouton.

Bucholtz, Mary, & Hall, Kira. (2005). Identity and interaction: A sociocultural linguistic approach. *Discourse Studies*, 7(4–5), 585–614.

Carroll, Noël. (1988). *Philosophical Problems of Classical Film Theory*. Princeton, NJ: Princeton University Press.

Chapman, Siobhan, & Clark, Billy (Eds.). (2014). *Pragmatic Literary Stylistics*. Basingstoke: Palgrave Macmillan.

Chapman, Siobhan, & Clark, Billy (Eds.). (2019). *Pragmatics and Literature*. Amsterdam: John Benjamins.

Clapp, Susannah. (2014). Hamlet review: Maxine Peake is a delicately ferocious Prince of Denmark. *The Guardian*, 21 September, https://bit.ly/3EF3a5z (last accessed 18 February 2022).

Clark, Herbert H., & Brennan, Susan E. (1991). Grounding in communication. In Lauren B. Resnick, John M. Levine, & Stephanie D. Teasley (Eds.), *Perspectives on Socially Shared Cognition* (pp. 407–12). Washington, DC: APA Books.

Clark, Herbert H., & Schaefer, Edward F. (1987). Collaborating on contributions to conversations. *Language and Cognitive Processes* 2(1), 19–41.

Cochrane, Leslie E. (2017). An imagined community of practice: Online discourse among wheelchair users. *Linguistics Online* 87(8), 151–66.

Corpus of Contemporary American English. (n.d.). www.english-corpora.org/coca/ (last accessed 30 November 2022).

Culpeper, Jonathan. (2001). *Language and Characterisation: People in Plays and other Texts*. London: Longman Pearson Education.

Culpeper, Jonathan, Short, Mick, & Verdonk, Peter (Eds.). (1998). *Exploring the Language of Drama. From Text to Context*. London: Routledge.

Davies, Bronwyn, & Harré, Rom. (1990). Positioning: The discursive production of selves. *Journal for the Theory of Social Behaviour* 20(1), 43–63.

Dayter, Daria. (2016). *Discursive Self in Microblogging: Speech Acts, Stories and Self-praise*. Amsterdam: John Benjamins.

Díaz-Cintas, Jorge, & Remael, Aline. (2007). *Audiovisual Translation: Subtitling*. New York: Routledge.

Dynel, Marta. (2011). 'You talking to me?' The viewer as a ratified listener to film discourse. *Journal of Pragmatics* 43(6), 1628–44.

Dynel, Marta. (2017). Participation as audience design. In Christian R. Hoffmann and Wolfram Bublitz (Eds.), *Pragmatics of Social Media* (Handbooks of Pragmatics 11) (pp. 61–82). Berlin: De Gruyter Mouton.

Eckert, Penelope, & McConnell-Ginet, Sally. (1992). Think practically and act locally: Language and gender as community-based practice. *Annual Review of Anthropology* 21, 461–90.

Fischer-Lichte, Erika. (2008). *The Transformative Power of Performance. A New Aesthetics*. Saskya Iris Jain (trans.). London: Routledge.

Fisher, Judith W. (2003). Audience participation in the eighteenth-century London theatre. In Susan Kattwinkel (Ed.), *Audience Participation. Essays on Inclusion in Performance* (pp. 55–69). Westport, CT: Praeger.

Flückiger, Barbara. (2001). *Sound Design: Die virtuelle Klangwelt des Films*. Marburg: Schüren Verlag.

Gavins, Joanna. (2007). *Text World Theory: An Introduction*. Edinburgh: Edinburgh University Press.

Gee, James Paul. (2005). Semiotic social spaces and affinity spaces: From *The Age of Mythology* to today's schools. In David Barton & Karin Tusting (Eds.), *Beyond Communities of Practice: Language Power and Social Context* (pp. 214–32). Cambridge: Cambridge University Press. https://:10.1017/CBO97805 11610554.012

Genette, Gérard. (1982). *Palimpsestes. La littérature au second degré*. Paris: Éditions du Seuil.

Genette, Gérard. (1997). *Paratexts: Thresholds of Interpretation. Literature, Culture, Theory*. Cambridge: Cambridge University Press.

Georgakopoulou, Alexandra. (2007). *Small Stories, Interaction and Identities*. Amsterdam: John Benjamins.

Goffman, Erving. (1979). Footing. *Semiotica* 25 (1–2), 1–29.

Guillot, Marie-Noëlle. (2017). Subtitling and dubbing in telecinematic text. In Miriam A. Locher & Andreas H. Jucker (Eds.), *Pragmatics of Fiction* (pp. 397–424). Berlin: De Gruyter Mouton.

Guillot, Marie-Noëlle. (2020). The pragmatics of audiovisual translation: Voices from within in film subtitling. *Journal of Pragmatics* 170, 317–30.

Harvard, Anna & Wahlberg, Katarina. (2017). *The Visual Guide to Improv*. Stockholm: International Theater Stockholm.

Hoffmann, Christian R. (2017). Narrative perspectives on voice in fiction. In Miriam A. Locher & Andreas H. Jucker (Eds.), *Pragmatics of Fiction* (pp. 159–95). Berlin: De Gruyter Mouton.

Jahn, Manfred. (2021). Narratology 2.3: A guide to the theory of narrative. English Department, University of Cologne. www.uni-koeln.de/~ame02/pppn.pdf (last accessed 6 December 2021).

Jucker, Andreas H. (2015) Pragmatics of fiction: Literary uses of *uh* and *um*. *Journal of Pragmatics* 86, 63–7.

Jucker, Andreas H. (2021). Features of orality in the language of fiction: A corpus-based investigation. *Language and Literature: International Journal of Stylistics* 30(4), 341–60.

Jucker, Andreas H., & Locher, Miriam A. (2017). Introducing *Pragmatics of Fiction*: Approaches, trends and developments. In Miriam A. Locher & Andreas H. Jucker (Eds.), *Pragmatics of Fiction* (pp. 1–21). Berlin: De Gruyter Mouton.

Kouta, Ashraf T. M. (2021). Narrative nonlinearity and the birth of the wreader: A hypertext critical reading of selected digital literary texts. *Critique: Studies in Contemporary Fiction* 62(5), 586–602.

Kozloff, Sarah. (2000). *Overhearing Film Dialogue*. Berkeley: University of California Press.

Kristeva, Julia. (1980 [1977]). Word, Dialogue, and Novel. In Leon S. Roudiez (Ed.), Thomas al (Trans.), *Desire in Language: Approach to Literature and Art* (pp. 64–91). New York: Columbia University Press.

Labov, William. (1972). *Language in the Inner City. Studies in the Black English Vernacular*. Philadelphia: University of Pennsylvania Press.

Landert, Daniela. (2021a). The spontaneous co-creation of comedy: Humour in improvised theatrical fiction. *Journal of Pragmatics* 173, 68–87.

Landert, Daniela. (2021b). Only one chance to make a first impression: Characterisation in the opening scenes of TV series pilot episodes. In Carmen Gregori-Signes, Miguel Fuster-Márquez, & Sergio Maruenda-Bataller (Eds.), *Discourse, Dialogue and Characterisation in TV Series* (pp. 109–126). Granada: Editorial Comares.

Landow, George P. (2006). *Hypertext 3.0: Critical Theory and New Media in an Era of Globalization*. Baltimore, MD: The John Hopkins University Press.

Lave, Jean, & Wenger, Etienne (1991). *Situated Learning: Legitimate Peripheral Participation*. Cambridge: Cambridge University Press.

Leech, Geoffrey N., & Short, Mick. (2007). *Style in Fiction. A Linguistic Introduction to English Fictional Prose* (2nd ed.). London: Routledge.

Locher, Miriam A. (2008). Relational work, politeness and identity construction. In Gerd Antos, Eija Ventola, & Tilo Weber (Eds.), *Handbooks of Applied Linguistics. Volume 2: Interpersonal Communication* (pp. 509–40). Berlin: Mouton de Gruyter.

Locher, Miriam A. (2017). Multilingualism in fiction. In Miriam A. Locher & Andreas H. Jucker (Eds.), *Pragmatics of Fiction* (pp. 297–327). Berlin: De Gruyter Mouton.

Locher, Miriam A. (2020). Moments of relational work in English fan translations of Korean TV drama. *Journal of Pragmatics* 170, 139–55.

Locher, Miriam A., & Jucker, Andreas H. (Eds.). (2017). *Pragmatics of Fiction*. Berlin: De Gruyter Mouton.

Locher, Miriam A., & Jucker, Andreas H. (2021). *The Pragmatics of Fiction. Literature, Stage and Screen Discourse*. Edinburgh: Edinburgh University Press.

Locher, Miriam A., & Messerli, Thomas C. (2020). Translating the other: Communal TV watching of Korean TV drama. *Journal of Pragmatics* 170, 20–36.

Locher, Miriam A., & Watts, Richard J. (2008). Relational work and impoliteness: Negotiating norms of linguistic behaviour. In Derek Bousfield & Miriam A. Locher (Eds.), *Impoliteness in Language. Studies on its Interplay with Power in Theory and Practice* (pp. 77–99). Berlin: Mouton de Gruyter.

Lösel, Gunter. (2013). *Das Spiel mit dem Chaos. Zur Performativität des Improvisationstheaters*. Bielefeld: transcript Verlag.

Love, Catherine. (2019). Hamlet review: This fresh prince is fully and gloriously female. *The Guardian*, 11 March 2019, https://bit.ly/3OHLgnh (last accessed 18 February 2022).

McDonough, Kim, Ammar, Ahlem, & Sellami, Amal (2021). L2 French students' conversations during interactive writing tasks and their interaction mindset. *Foreign Language Annals* 55(1), 222–36.

Messerli, Thomas C. (2016). Extradiegetic and character laughter as markers of humorous intentions in the sitcom *2 Broke Girls*. *Journal of Pragmatics* 95, 79–92.

Messerli, Thomas C. (2017). Participation structure in fictional discourse: Authors, scriptwriters, audiences and characters. In Miriam A. Locher & Andreas H. Jucker (Eds.), *Pragmatics of Fiction* (pp. 25–54). Berlin: De Gruyter Mouton.

Messerli, Thomas C. (2019). Subtitles and cinematic meaning-making: Interlingual subtitles as textual agents. *Multilingua* 38(5), 529–46.

Messerli, Thomas C. (2020). Subtitled artefacts as communication: The case of *Ocean's Eleven* Scene 12. *Perspectives* 28(6), 851–63.

Messerli, Thomas C. (2021). *Repetition in Telecinematic Humour: How US American Sitcoms Employ Formal and Semantic Repetition in the Construction of Multimodal Humour.* Freiburg: Albert-Ludwigs-Universität Freiburg. https://bit.ly/3ui2H4r (last accessed 2 December 2022).

Messerli, Thomas C., & Locher, Miriam A. (2021). Humour support and emotive stance in comments on K-Drama. *Journal of Pragmatics* 178, 408–25.

Mittell, Jason. (2015). *Complex TV. The Poetics of Contemporary Television Storytelling.* New York: New York University Press.

Norrthon, Stefan. (2019). To stage an overlap: The longitudinal, collaborative and embodied process of staging eight lines in a professional theatre rehearsal process. *Journal of Pragmatics* 142, 171–84.

Oh, Youjeong. (2015). The interactive nature of Korean TV drama. Flexible texts, discursive consumption, and social media. In Sangjoon Lee & Markus Nornes (Eds.), *Hallyu 2.0: The Korean Wave in the Age of Social Media* (pp. 133–53). Ann Arbor: University of Michigan Press.

Olin-Scheller, Christina, & Wikström, Patrik. (2010). Literary prosumers: Young people's reading and writing. *Education Inquiry* 1(1), 41–56.

Pao, Angela C. (2010). *No Safe Spaces. Re-casting Race, Ethnicity, and Nationality in American Theater.* Ann Arbor: The University of Michigan Press.

Piazza, Roberta, Bednarek, Monika, & Rossi, Fabio (Eds.). (2011). *Telecinematic Discourse. Approaches to the Language of Films and Television Series.* Amsterdam: John Benjamins.

Planchenault, Gaëlle. (2017). Doing dialects in dialogues: Regional, social and ethnic variation in fiction. In Miriam A. Locher & Andreas H. Jucker (Eds.), *Pragmatics of Fiction* (pp. 265–96). Berlin: De Gruyter Mouton.

Queen, Robin. (2004). 'Du hast jar keene Ahnung': African American English dubbed into German. *Journal of Sociolinguistics* 8(4), 515–37.

Radulovic, Petrana. (2022). Netflix's interactive specials, ranked by how much your choices matter. From the trivia-based Cat Burglar to the Minecraft special that defines the field. *Polygon*, February 24. https://bit.ly/3u1T369 (last accessed 30 November 2022).

Reason, Matthew. (2015). Participations on participation: Researching the 'active' theatre audience. *Participations: Journal of Audience and Reception Studies* 12(1), 271–80.

Rebora, Simone, Boot, Peter, Pianzola, Federico, et al. (2021). Digital humanities and digital social reading. *Digital Scholarship in the Humanities* 36(2), ii230–50.

Rimmon-Kenan, Shlomith. (2002). *Narrative Fiction. Contemporary Poetics.* Second edition. London: Routledge.

Sawyer, Keith. (2003). *Improvised Dialogues. Emergence and Creativity in Conversation.* London: Ablex.

Schirra, Steven, Sun, Huan, & Bentley, Frank. (2014). *Together Alone: Motivations for Live-Tweeting a Television Series.* Paper presented at the CHI 2014 Proceedings of the SIGCHI Conference on Human Factors in Computing Systems, Toronto. https://doi.org/10.1145/2556288.2557070.

Schlütz, Daniela, & Jage-D'Aprile, Friederike. (2021). Audience engagement with spreadable texts: How to measure fan involvement with Game of Thrones. *Participations: Journal of Audience and Reception Studies* 18(2), 335–55.

Semino, Elena, & Short, Mick. (2004). *Corpus Stylistics: Speech, Writing and Thought Presentation in a Corpus of English Writing.* London: Routledge.

Stockwell, Peter, & Whiteley, Sara (Eds.). (2014). *The Cambridge Handbook of Stylistics.* Cambridge: Cambridge University Press.

The Guardian. (2019). Thy name is woman: Female Hamlets from Sarah Bernhardt to Cush Jumbo – In pictures. *The Guardian*, 29 May. https://bit .ly/3Ub6hIo (last accessed 18 February 2022).

Toolan, Michael. (2011). 'I don't know what they're saying half the time, but I'm hooked on the series': Incomprehensible dialogue and integrated multi-modal characterisation in *The Wire*. In Roberta Piazza, Monika Bednarek, & Fabio Rossi (Eds.), *Telecinematic Discourse. Approaches to the Language of Films and Television Series* (pp. 161–183). Amsterdam: John Benjamins.

Vandelanotte, Lieven. (2009). *Speech and Thought Representation in English: A Cognitive-Functional Approach.* Berlin: Mouton de Gruyter.

Watts, Richard J. (2008). Grammar writers in eighteenth-century Britain: A community of practice or a discourse community? In Ingrid Tieken Boon van Ostade (Ed.), *Grammars, Grammarians and Grammar-Writing in Eighteenth-Century England* (pp. 37–56). Berlin: De Gruyter Mouton.

Weaving, Simon, Pelzer, Sandra, & Adam, Marc T. P. (2018). The cinematic moment: Improving audience testing of movies. *Studies in Australasian Cinema* 12(2–3), 89–103.

Wenger, Etienne. (2002). *Communities of Practice: Learning, Meaning and Identity.* Cambridge: Cambridge University Press.

Zhang, Leticia Tian, & Cassany, Daniel. (2019a). 'The murderer is him ✓'. *Internet Pragmatics* 4(2), 272–94.

Zhang, Leticia Tian, & Cassany, Daniel. (2019b). The 'danmu' phenomenon and media participation: Intercultural understanding and language learning through 'The Ministry of Time'. *Comunicar* 27(58), 19–29.

Acknowledgements

The authors of this Element have a long-standing collaboration history working in pairs. For this work, we have worked as a group of four authors for the first time, which was both challenging as well as fun and creative, leading to a result that is different and (we hope) better than if we had written on our own. Daniela wishes to acknowledge funding through the SNF PRIMA grant PR00P1_185737/1, and she thanks Ilenia Tonetti Tübben, Sophie Rosset and Shannon Hughes for their help with recording and transcribing the performances from which the examples and insights on improvisation theatre are drawn, as well as the improvisation companies that allowed her to record and use the data (see references). Daniela's work on this Element was conducted at the University of Basel as well as at the Heidelberg University. Miriam wishes to thank the University of Basel for financing a research leave in spring 2022 and Korea University in Seoul for hosting her during the writing period of this book. We thank the anonymous reviewers and general editors for their constructive feedback, which helped to strengthen our line of argumentation. This open access manuscript has been published with the support of the Swiss National Science Foundation.

Funding Statement

Published with the support of the Swiss National Science Foundation.

Cambridge Elements

Pragmatics

Jonathan Culpeper
Lancaster University, UK

Jonathan Culpeper is Professor of English Language and Linguistics in the Department of Linguistics and English Language at Lancaster University, UK. A former co-editor-in-chief of the *Journal of Pragmatics* (2009–14), with research spanning multiple areas within pragmatics, his major publications include: *Impoliteness: Using Language to Cause Offence* (2011, CUP) and *Pragmatics and the English Language* (2014, Palgrave; with Michael Haugh).

Michael Haugh
University of Queensland, Australia

Michael Haugh is Professor of Linguistics and Applied Linguistics in the School of Languages and Cultures at the University of Queensland, Australia. A former co-editor-in-chief of the *Journal of Pragmatics* (2015–2020), with research spanning multiple areas within pragmatics, his major publications include: *Understanding Politeness* (2013, CUP; with Dániel Kádár), *Pragmatics and the English Language* (2014, Palgrave; with Jonathan Culpeper), and *Im/politeness Implicatures* (2015, Mouton de Gruyter).

Advisory Board

About the Series

Cambridge Elements in Pragmatics showcases dynamic and high-quality original, concise and accessible scholarly works. Written for a broad pragmatics readership, it encourages dialogue across different perspectives on language use. It is a forum for cutting-edge work in pragmatics: consolidating theory, leading the development of new methods, and advancing innovative topics in the field.

Cambridge Elements ☰

Pragmatics

Printed in the United States
by Baker & Taylor Publisher Services